Praises For
A Way of Escape

A Way of Escape describes a Bible-based approach to help deliver Christians from the bondage of porn and its related practices and sexual acts. "Walk in the Spirit and ye shall not fulfill the lust of the flesh" is the key verse (Galatians 5:16).

Porn appeals to the "lust of the flesh and the lust of the eyes" so common in the world today (I John 2:16a). Many Christians caught up in porn are hesitant to seek the help offered by Accountability Partner/Group interactions, perhaps for fear that information about participants might be leaked out. It is essential that believers find help through the power of the Holy Spirit to crucify the flesh with its affections and lusts (Galatians 5:24).

The battle plan described in this book has been successfully applied. It provides fresh hope for deliverance from porn and its many devastating effects. I highly recommend this book to those who feel trapped and hopelessly bound by porn.

Dr. Noel Caldwell, retired Engineer/Educator, and Ordained Minister

***

Wiley Graf writes from the personal experience of his own struggle with pornography. He depicts it as a battle between the flesh and the Spirit.

He does a great job of pointing out the need for a Spirit-filled life to enable us to successfully win that battle. I would encourage you to saturate your mind with the truths he brings out in this book. And then put them into practice.

Bob Combs, Pastor Emeritus, Norton Grace Church

***

A Way of Escape offers an important message of hope, especially needed in these trying times. Readers are given a practical plan for gaining victory over any addiction, and are reminded that they are never alone in their struggle. This book will set many people free.

Bob Harmelink, President, Matthew Publishing

***

First of all, I love the title of the book *A Way of Escape* taken directly from I Corinthians 10:13. It's a very unique approach for overcoming sexual sins. The author states how not to ignore the red flags, and sweep sins under the carpet of "positional truth." "Walking in the Spirit" is the key to victory. And the author goes into detail describing what this "Walking in the Spirit" scripturally means.

I especially appreciate the author's honesty in references to his own personal struggles and to his finding shelter in Ephesians 5:18b-19. The run-to-safety applications of "living in the Spirit" often come in the form of singing songs, hymns, and spiritual songs.

Gary LaFollette, Worship Pastor

A WAY OF ESCAPE

A Spirit-Powered Battle Plan for Purity
(Accountability Partner/Group *Not* Required!)

Wiley Graf, PhD

For those longing with all their heart to be clean but still desperately struggling to find a way of escape.

And, of course,

... to Him who is able to do exceedingly abundantly above all that we ask or think, according to the power that works in us, To Him be glory in the Church by Christ Jesus to all generations, forever and ever. Amen.
(Ephesians 3:20-21)

Author's Note

This publication is sold with the understanding that the author is not engaged in rendering psychological, legal, or other professional services. If expert assistance or counseling is needed, the services of a competent professional should be sought.

The information and results provided in this publication are based solely on the author's personal experience. Every individual is different. Results reported by the author in no way constitute a guarantee of similar results for the reader.

ACKNOWLEDGEMENTS

A special thanks to each of the following. This work truly would not have been possible without their contributions.

Mr. Dale C. Saylor, pastor of Men's Ministry at The Chapel in Green, OH, for taking the time to read the manuscript, for your always timely words of encouragement, and for writing the First Foreword.

Bill and Gloria Gaither, and all of their Homecoming Friends, for faithfully exercising their spiritual gifts. What vision in building a ministry (the Homecoming concert series) that will still be positively impacting lives long after we are all called Home. You are the embodiment of Ephesians 5:18b-19. And untold numbers are the beneficiaries thereof. Well done, Bill and Gloria Gaither!

And finally, to everyone at Kharis Publishing for believing in this book, and its fresh take on the Holy Spirit, and His power to do exceedingly abundantly above all that we ask or think (Ephesians 3:20). A special thanks to Prof. Francis E. Umesiri and Mr. James Clement for "finding" me and my book at christianbookproposals.com. And to Heather for making the final corrections and edits to the manuscript.

TABLE OF CONTENTS

Counterattack Measures
(and Six Observations)

Six Observations

JUMP-START READING GUIDE

Is this book for you? Is it worth investing roughly 10 hours of your valuable time to read in its entirety?

Readers can gain a quick feel for the book's content and originality by sampling excerpts of varying sizes. Excerpts requiring from as little as several minutes to several hours to read.

The Six KEYS to Escape (6 minutes): The quickest read of the excerpts, the KEYS to Escape provide the reader with six key Scripture-based insights into the inner-working power of the Holy Spirit to deliver believers from lusts of the flesh.

- KEY VERSE (page 64)
- KEY REGULARITY (page 65)
- KEY IMPOSSIBILITY (page 67)
- KEY INSIGHT (page 68)
- KEY Connect-the-Verses FLOWCHART (page 109)
- KEY SIMPLIFICATION (page 165)

83 Boldface Italicized Theme Statements (60 minutes): The boldface italicized theme statements provide the reader with another relatively quick means of determining whether they want to read the book in its entirety. Intimately familiar with the book's content, I (the author) am able to read and digest content of the 83 theme statements in approximately 10 minutes. Double the time for readers less familiar with the book's content. And triple that time for those wishing to browse the text immediately preceding and following each theme statement (10 minutes x 2 x 3 = 60 minutes).

50 Selected Pages (2-1/2 hours): The basic content of Chapters 1-5 is not new. For the reader only interested in gaining a quick feel for the book's originality, these five chapters may be skipped initially. Similarly, portions of Chapter 7 and seven of the eight Appendices may also be skipped initially. Only material that yields insight into the book's originality is included in the following reading list of selected chapters:

- First Foreword ....2 pages
- Author Foreword 7
- Chapter 6 9
- Chapter 7, pages 71-77 and 102-109 15
- Chapter 8 9
- Chapter 9 3
- Chapter 10 2
- Appendix G 3

TOTAL   50 pages

Assuming a leisurely rate of three minutes per page, one ought to be able to read and digest content of these 50 pages in about 2-1/2 hours.

Whole Book (< 10 hours): Each of the excerpts struck a chord. This is a must-read. Again assuming a leisurely rate of three minutes per page, one ought to be able to read and digest content of the entire 190-page book in less than 10 hours.

FIRST FOREWORD

Brain experts have not yet determined the limits of the brain's abilities. Some believe that we may never fully understand them. But strong evidence does support the existence of one of its most important processes: neuroplasticity.

"Neuroplasticity" refers to the brain's ability to restructure or rewire itself when it recognizes the need for adaption. This is the premise that the author [Wiley Graf] uses to essentially overcome or rewire a brain that is addicted to pornography.

In reading Galatians 5:16-25, we are encouraged to "walk" by the Spirit, be "led" by the Spirit, "Bear the fruit" of the Spirit, "Live" by the Spirit, and "keep in step" with the Spirit. We must acknowledge that, on our own, we are incapable of dealing with the pressures of the world. This "brain rewiring" is a daily requirement of leaning hard on the assistance provided by the Holy Spirit.

I am proud of Wiley for sharing his experience. And for the encouragement he provides to readers of his book, *A Way of Escape.*

Dale C. Saylor

Pastor—Men's Ministry, The Chapel in Green
Retired Teacher—20-plus years teaching psychology and sociology
classes in the Ohio public school system

AUTHOR FOREWORD

The purpose of this work is to set forth a Spirit-powered Battle Plan for living pure in an impure, porn/sex-crazed world.

The book's title is taken from I Corinthians 10:13. God, who cannot lie, has promised His children that there is a way of escape from every temptation. He adds no disclaimers or exceptions. His promises extend to every age, even to ours, corrupted as it is by the many forms of easily accessible pornography.

Problem Statement: There is a battle going on between the flesh and the Spirit (Galatians 5:17a). For far too many in the Church, the flesh is winning. Before the Spirit can even cry, "Incoming!", the flesh is already at work, causing the Christian to behave in ways that are contrary to the Spirit (Galatians 5:17b). Having been overcome so often, the war-weary Christian cries out to God, "What am I to do? I've prayed. I've fasted. I've memorized Scripture. And still I fail. You promised a way of escape. Where is it? What is it?"

> *For the flesh lusts against the Spirit, and the Spirit against the flesh; and these are contrary to one another, so that you do not do the things that you*

wish (Galatians 5:17).

Let us begin by acknowledging that there is a problem. A study involving over 3000 persons revealed that 60-70% of men, 50-58% of pastors, and 20-30% of women in evangelical churches suffer from some form of sexual addiction.[1] Addictions covered a broad spectrum of sexual sins including sexual fantasy, masturbation, viewing pornography, and engaging in sexual activities outside of the marriage covenant.[2] Numbers will certainly vary with pollster, definition of addiction, and respondent classification (e.g., self-identified vs. practicing Christian, and definition of the latter). Still, it seems safe to conclude that, in this age of Internet pornography, sexual addiction is a very real problem in today's Church.

> *60-70% of men, 50-58% of pastors, and 20-30% of women in evangelical churches suffer from some form of sexual addiction.[1]*

A Proposed Solution: If this were a battle between armies of two warring nations, the besieged nation, far from surrendering, could even turn the tide of battle back into its favor. First, instead of waiting for an attack, it could launch pre-emptive strikes against the aggressor nation before it had an opportunity to gain full strength. Not only would this reduce the number of "incomings," but the now-weakened enemy's subsequent attacks would likely be of reduced strength. Second, it could also train crack units of special operations agents and have them ready to "take out" the enemy on those now much rarer occasions when it did still manage to break through.

These same warring options are available to Christians in their battle with the flesh. The genuinely born-again believer, in whom the Holy Spirit resides, possesses all the weapons necessary to turn the tide of battle back into his favor:

- **Pre-Emptive Strikes**: Reduce both the number and strength of enemy "incomings" by launching Bible-based, pre-emptive strikes against the flesh, while it is yet in a relatively weakened state (Chapters 3-5)
- **Counterattack Measures**: Call on crack units of special operations agents, particularly strong in the Spirit, to "take out" the flesh on those now much rarer occasions

when it does still manage to break through (Chapters 6-7, however, these special agents are also deployed quite extensively in pre-emptive mode)

What's New? Why another book on living sexually pure, when other authors and purity programs are already reporting great success in Christian circles? What differentiates this work from those that have gone before? There are five primary distinctive:

1. **Limbic Weaponry (Chapter 2)**: Emphasis is placed on using highly emotional, highly visual spiritual weaponry in the war against the flesh.

The limbic system is the brain's seat of emotions and an input receiver for the senses (think emotional, visual). Imprints of the images the porn addict has viewed are also stored in memory in the limbic system. It is here therefore, in the limbic system, that most of the battle for the brain takes place. For healing to occur, the limbic system must be accessed and the brain reprogrammed.[3,4]

When the flesh mounts a sensual (strongly emotional), image-laden (strongly visual) attack and the addict's counterattack is a words-only prayer or memory verse (lightly emotional, non-visual), the result is predictably bad. Why? Because, at best, the latter only lightly engages the brain's limbic system. But if the counterattack combines words with spiritually-and-emotionally-charged imagery, the brain is engaged in a much more powerful way, and the flesh can be repelled.

> *If the counterattack combines words with spiritually-and-emotionally-charged imagery, the brain is engaged in a much more powerful way, and the flesh can be repelled.*

2. **Walking in the Spirit (Chapter 6)**: Walking in the Spirit is the key to discovering God's promised way of escape from temptation.

God has promised that there is a way of escape from every temptation (I Corinthians 10:13). Appealing to a second promise of Scripture, in the *Way of Escape* Battle Plan, the Holy Spirit is charged with leading the escape (Galatians 5:16). Integral to this plan is construction of a library of Spirit-anointed, flesh-diffusing apps, custom-fitted to the believer and his unique Spirit-filling triggers (Ephesians 5:18b-19). Escape, compliments of the Holy Spirit!

> *I say then: Walk in the Spirit, and you shall not fulfill the lust of the flesh (Galatians 5:16).*

3. **Active Pursuit of Regular Relationship Intimacy with the Holy Spirit (Chapter 6)**: The active pursuit of regular relationship intimacy with the Holy Spirit is the key to unleashing His inner-working power (Ephesians 3:20) and winning the war against the flesh.

Most believers have only a passive relationship with the Holy Spirit. They know Him, alright. They were fully indwelt by Him at conversion, of course. But only occasionally do they now experience relationship intimacy with Him. Something the pastor said in Sunday's sermon tugged on their heart. The week before it was the choir's rendition of a favorite hymn that left them teary-eyed. And last month there were those moving testimonies during the baptismal service. All resulted in intimate encounters with the Holy Spirit. But all were spaced days or even weeks apart. And, as is usually the case, all were *passive*. All were dependent on the Spirit to initiate the encounter. Most believers rarely think (or even know why they might want) to initiate an intimate encounter with the Holy Spirit.

The *Way of Escape* Battle Plan is all about initiating intimate encounters with the Holy Spirit. And not only on Sunday mornings while seated in a church pew. A daily filling of the Spirit. Or even multiple times a day. As often as the sheltering presence of the Spirit is needed in the war against the flesh. The active pursuit of regular relationship intimacy with the Holy Spirit. This is what sets the *Way of Escape* Battle Plan apart from all other battle plans.

> *The active pursuit of regular relationship intimacy with the Holy Spirit. This is what sets the* Way of Escape *Battle Plan apart from all other battle plans.*

4. **Dramatic Drop in Enemy Attacks (Chapter 8)**: The
   flesh's attack capability is severely compromised by
   regular viewing of the Spirit-anointed, flesh-diffusing
   apps *in pre-emptive mode*, while the flesh is yet in a relatively
   weakened state.

Dropping the passivity, and taking the battle to the flesh, reduced
enemy "incomings" to approximately one-fifth of pre-book numbers
(see *Real Data*, Chapter 8). The Spirit-anointed apps create healthy neural
pathways that deepen each time the app is viewed, while, according to
the neurological principle of use-it-or-lose-it, the unhealthy, now-idle
fleshly pathways are pruned back. Science has finally caught up with Holy
Scripture. The Bible declared these neurological principles nearly 2000
years ago:

> *Therefore submit to God. Resist the devil and he will*
> *flee from you. Draw near to God and He will draw*
> *near to you … (James 4:7-8a)*

Each time I resist the devil, I am breaking unhealthy neural
pathways. In the spiritual realm, the devil is indeed fleeing. And each time
I choose to draw near to God, I am creating/deepening healthier neural
pathways. In the spiritual realm, God is indeed drawing nearer.

The spectacular success of the Spirit-anointed, pre-emptive strikes
gives rise to a fifth distinctive:

5. **Accountability Group Not Required (Chapters 6-10)**:
   By tapping into the Holy Spirit's power to deliver from
   lusts of the flesh (Galatians 5:16), mind renewal is
   possible without ever having to enlist the aid of an
   accountability partner or group.

This fifth distinctive is huge. All Christian authors and purity
programs that I have reviewed insist that this is a battle that cannot be
won alone. If it is to be successful, an accountability partner/group must
be part of the recovery program. In support of this position, Scripture
passages encouraging the confession of sin to a fellow Christian are often
cited (e.g., Galatians 6:1-2, James 5:16), as are the added benefits of
building community and stronger churches.

Despite these strong and convincing arguments, I suspect that the thought of confessing sexual sins in a group setting will cause most Christian men to quit a program before they even get started. Even if this were the only available option, I suspect that most Christian men would still choose to hoist the white flag, acknowledge defeat, and resign themselves to a hypocritical, inconsistent walk, conceding that, "This is just a part of who I am, and I will never be able to completely shake this addiction." They likely take comfort in knowing that they are only "sometimes" inconsistent. And may even cite passages like Romans 7:17-25 and Galatians 5:17 to mistakenly justify their inconsistent walk. Many more would be willing to give purity programs a try, if they were not required to become part of an accountability group. It is for this still-struggling, still quietly suffering group of Christian men that this book was written.

Now imagine the impact of a Battle Plan for purity that would allow the *individual* Christian—apart from an accountability group—to escape temptation, even in those moments when the flesh is banging down the door. This work proposes to offer just such a Battle Plan, with "walking in the Spirit" its key component and Spirit-anointed, limbic weaponry (think emotional, visual) the fast-acting catalyst of spiritual reaction.

> *In the* **Way of Escape** *Battle Plan, "walking in the Spirit" is the key component and Spirit-anointed, limbic weaponry (think emotional, visual) the fast-acting catalyst of spiritual reaction.*

The still-struggling now have another option. The still-struggling now have fresh hope for discovering that long-sought-after way of escape (I Corinthians 10:13). A way that does not require enlisting the aid of an accountability partner or group.

> *... but God is faithful, who will not allow you to be tempted beyond what you are able, but with the temptation will also make the WAY OF ESCAPE, that you may be able to bear it (I Corinthians 10:13).*

A Few Final Comments Before Plunging In: I suspect that most Christians (author included) fighting this battle are not engaging in sexual activities outside of the marriage covenant. Their struggle revolves primarily around the viewing of pornography. And so, while aware that sexual addiction covers a much broader spectrum of sexual sins, throughout the text, I will often narrow the focus of addiction discussions to struggles related to the viewing of pornography.

The startling statistic concerning women notwithstanding (e.g., 20-30% of women in evangelical churches suffer from some form of sexual addiction[1]), throughout the text, I have chosen to always use masculine pronouns in discussions pertaining to the plight of the porn/sex addict. There is, however, also every reason to believe that the *Way of Escape* Battle Plan can be just as effective in helping women combat their sexual addictions.

The information and results provided herein are based solely on my personal experience. And while I heartily believe others will benefit from the *Way of Escape* Battle Plan, the results that I report in no way constitute a guarantee of similar results for the reader.

In closing, know that I regularly pray that my readers might also discover God's promised way of escape. A way that is uniquely fitted to their history and circumstances, and their unique Spirit-filling triggers.

Wiley Graf
January 31, 2022

INTRODUCTION

Moreover, brethren, I do not want you to be unaware that all our fathers were under the cloud, all passed through the sea, All were baptized into Moses in the cloud and in the sea, All ate the same spiritual food, And all drank the same spiritual drink. For they drank of that spiritual Rock that followed them, and that Rock was Christ. But with most of them God was not well pleased, for their bodies were scattered in the wilderness. Now these things became our examples, to the intent that we should not lust after evil things as they also lusted. And do not become idolaters as were some of them. As it is written, "The people sat down to eat and drink, and rose up to play." Nor let us commit sexual immorality, as some of them did, and in one day twenty-three thousand fell; Nor let us tempt Christ, as some of them also tempted, and were destroyed by serpents; Nor complain, as some of them also complained, and were destroyed by the destroyer. Now all these things happened to them as examples, and they were written for our admonition, upon whom the ends of the ages have come. Therefore let him who thinks he stands take heed lest he fall. No temptation has overtaken you except such as is

**common to man; but God is faithful, who will not allow you to be
tempted beyond what you are able, but with the temptation will
also make *the way of escape*, that you may be able to bear it
(I Corinthians 10:1-13).**

WRITTEN FOR OUR INSTRUCTION

The title for this book (*italicized* above) is taken from I Corinthians
10:13. The church in Corinth was riddled with sin—some so great that
they were not even named among the heathen (I Corinthians 5:1).
Against this backdrop, Paul writes of God's great promise of deliverance
from temptation. But prior to getting to the promised way of escape in
verse 13, we must first wade through 12 verses of warnings to the
Corinthians concerning their ongoing sins. Mankind does not change.
We are prone to making the same mistakes. Paul's warnings to the church
at Corinth were written for our admonition (instruction) as well.

> *Mankind does not change. We are prone to making
> the same mistakes. Paul's warnings to the church at
> Corinth were written for our instruction as well.*

In warning the Corinthians, Paul did not draw from the failings of
the spiritually ignorant heathen. No, the failings that he described were
of the elect of Israel. Those persons that had been blessed with
knowledge of the One True God. Persons that had eaten and drank of
that spiritual Rock that was Christ (v. 1-4). Despite their privileged
position, many of the children of Israel had allowed gross sin back into
their lives. They thought that they were still okay (v. 12). But God was
not well-pleased with most (v. 5a). His displeasure was tangibly measured
by the great number that perished in the wilderness (v. 5b), never having
seen nor having set foot in the Promised Land.

Paul bookends specifics of the Israelite's sins with this
explanation—he is relating their sad story, and citing their specific sins
so that his readers (including modern-day Christians) would not make
the same mistakes (v. 6, 11). Despite having been blessed with knowledge
of the One True God, they continued to lust after evil things (v. 6),
practice idolatry (v. 7), engage in sexually immoral activities (v. 8), tempt
God/Christ (v. 9), and complain (v. 10). Lives characterized by these
(and other) wicked practices should have been red-flag indicators for the

Israelites that God was not well-pleased with them (v. 5a).

Finally, after 12 verses of warnings, comes the desperately needed promise of escape. No matter how strong temptation's hold might now be, God has promised a way of escape. I am not to follow the example of the Israelites, hoist the white flag, and surrender to temptation. I am not to ignore the red flags and sweep my sins under the carpet of "positional truth." If it was God's design for His people to be only "positionally pure," why was He so displeased with the many that had fallen into gross sin (v. 5a)? Or, if God's displeasure was limited to only Old Testament persons, why was Paul using these examples in a New Testament epistle?

God's promised way of escape is not a "positional truth." Nor are Scripture's warnings applicable to only Old Testament persons. He has promised very real ways of escape from all forms of temptation. And New Testament Christians, if they are to be well-pleasing to God (v. 5a), are to earnestly pursue them.

SEXUAL ADDICTION

God promises a way of escape from all temptations common to man (v. 13a). To simplify matters moving forward, in our discussions of God's promised way of escape, the focus will be on temptations associated with sexual addictions, defined as follows:

> *Sexual addiction refers to a broad spectrum of sexual sins which a person cannot break. To name a few, the person who cannot stop watching pornography, masturbating, having sexual fantasies, or engaging in sexual activities outside of the marriage covenant, is most likely in sexual bondage.[1]*

"What does this have to do with the Church?" some might naively ask. Sad to say, but sexual addictions, as defined above, are no stranger to the twenty-first century Church. Consider this startling statistic:

> *A study involving over 3000 persons revealed that 60-70% of men, 50-58% of pastors, and 20-30% of women in evangelical churches suffer from some form of sexual addiction.[2]*

Numbers will certainly vary with pollster, definition of addiction, and respondent classification (e.g., self-identified vs. practicing Christian, and definition of the latter). Still, it seems safe to conclude that, in this age of Internet pornography, sexual addiction is a very real problem in today's Church.

The Israelites were no more righteous than the peoples of the surrounding nations. God simply required a nation to "declare His glory among the nations, His wonders among all peoples" (I Chronicles 16:24), and He chose Israel to be that nation. But when mired in sins, some even more grievous than their less-enlightened neighbors (I Corinthians 5:1), the Israelites could no longer be effective witnesses to God's glory. In like manner, the twenty-first century Church, mired in sexual sins just as grievous as their less-enlightened neighbors, can no longer be salt and light to a lost and dying world so desperately in need of Christ.

Few would deny that the Church's overall influence is on the decline. Real (vs. positional) change is required if this trend is to be reversed. Real escape from sexual sins is a necessary first step.

IF GOD SAYS THERE IS A WAY OF ESCAPE

... but God is faithful, who will not allow you to be tempted beyond what you are able, but with the temptation will also make *the way of escape*, that you may be able to bear it (I Corinthians 10:13).

Matthew Maury Took God at His Word: Confined to bed during an illness, naval officer Matthew Fontaine Maury (1806-1873) had his son read to him from the Bible each evening. On one occasion, his son read from the eighth Psalm. When he came to the eighth verse, Maury had his son re-read it several times:

The birds of the air, and the fish of the sea that pass through the paths of the seas (Psalm 8:8).

Finally, the senior Maury said, "If God says there are paths in the sea, I am going to find them."

... Maury said, "If God says there are paths in the

28

sea, I am going to find them."

Nicknamed "Pathfinder of the Seas," Maury made many contributions to charting the seasonal winds and ocean currents, including the charting of ocean lanes for passing ships at sea. His 1847 publication of the *Wind and Current Charts of the North Atlantic* showed navigators how to use currents and winds to their advantage to reduce the time required for ocean voyages. His system of recording oceanographic data was adopted by navies and merchant marines around the world and was used to develop charts for all of the major trade routes. By following Maury's directions, the average 55-day voyage from New York-to-Rio de Janeiro was reduced to 35 days (40 days upon returning). His entire story is recounted in *Matthew Fontaine Maury: The Pathfinder of the Seas.*[3]

Let Us Also Take God at His Word: How often have I heard a dear brother in the faith—in a tired and weary voice—admit to living the life of a hypocrite? He had doubtless attempted to escape sin's grip many times but had failed on each occasion; the resignation in his voice indicating that he had likely stopped trying. His hopes for purity dashed, he now clings to passages like Romans 7:17-25 and Galatians 5:17 to wrongly justify his inconsistent, hypocritical walk.

Dear Christian brother: Do not give up hope. Do not hoist the white flag, and give in to temptation. Do not be content with being a statistic (e.g., 60-70% of men ... in evangelical churches suffer from some form of sexual addiction.[2]). If God says that there is a way of escape, we can be certain that there is. Let's go find it!

> *If God says that there is a way of escape, we can be*
> *certain that there is. Let's go find it!*

Matthew Maury took God at His Word and was rewarded with his discovery of the paths of the sea. If we will also take God at His Word and diligently seek His promised way of escape from sexual sin, might we not also be rewarded with its discovery?

WHERE WE'RE HEADED

In every believer, there is an ongoing battle between the flesh and the Spirit (Galatians 5:17). The flesh, well aware of the believer's weaknesses, is constantly on the prowl, looking for opportunities to pounce. Quite the different dynamic is playing out with the Spirit. Most believers have only a passive relationship with Him. As a result, most have never learned how to press the issue and bring the Spirit's mightiest weapons to bear in this battle.

The *Way of Escape* Battle Plan proposes to change this dynamic. Believers are provided with a set of Bible-based, Spirit-powered strike options for taking the battle to the flesh:

- **Pre-Emptive Strikes**: Drop the passivity. Launch a series of Bible-based, pre-emptive strikes to keep the flesh in a relatively weakened state, reducing both the number and strength of enemy "incomings."
- **Counterattack Measures**: Bring in crack units of special operations agents, particularly strong in the Spirit, to "take out" the flesh on those now rarer occasions when it does manage to still break through.

Pre-Emptive Strikes: There is much the believer can do while the flesh is still in a relatively weakened state. Attacks of the flesh can be greatly reduced in both number and strength if the believer drops the passivity and launches a series of Bible-based, pre-emptive strikes:

- Fill large blocks of idle time with ministries that exercise the gifts of the Spirit (Chapter 3)
- Trash all pornographic material, and either protect or eliminate (preferred) all electronic devices that could potentially offend the eyes (Chapter 4)
- Watch and pray over those times and places where the flesh has launched attacks in the past (Chapter 5)

Once launched, these three Scripture-based, pre-emptive strikes leave the flesh with much less time/opportunity to wreak havoc. These options for tilting the battlefield in the Spirit's favor are described in greater detail in Chapters 3-5.

Attacks of the flesh, though much reduced in number by these pre-emptive strikes, will still eventually come. Turning back the flesh when it is at full strength will not be as easy. The pre-emptive strike options of Chapters 3-5 will no longer be effective against the flesh once it is raging. But there are still very effective counterattack options available to the believer for those now rarer occasions when the flesh does still manage to break through.

Counterattack Measures: When he does now occasionally break through, special forces, particularly strong in the Spirit, can be mobilized to "take out" the flesh. Trained to be always "walking in the Spirit" (Chapter 6), these special forces correspond to the flesh-diffusing applications that directly issue in a filling of the Spirit (Chapter 7).

Before describing the three pre-emptive strike options (Chapters 3-5), recent advances in neuroscience are reviewed. While it almost always begins as a moral problem, sexual addiction is also very much a brain problem.[4] A better understanding of this dynamic is critical for developing a successful Spirit-led Escape Plan.

NOTE: The phrase "attacks of the flesh" appears twice in this chapter. The related phrase "acting out" (and variations thereof) will appear in future chapters. Definitions are in order.

God created man as a sexual being. Not every sexual desire is an attack of the flesh. It is natural for a man to experience sexual desire for his wife. Throughout this book, the phrase "attacks of the flesh" refers only to those times when the flesh is urging sexual release via: (i) masturbation—with or without the use of pornographic material, or (ii) sexual relations outside of the marriage covenant. A man "acts out" sexually when he acts upon these urges by following through to sexual release.

THE NEUROLOGY OF ADDICTION

For I know that in me (that is, in my flesh) nothing good dwells; for to will is present with me, but how to perform what is good I do not find. For the good that I will to do, I do not do; but the evil I will not to do, that I practice … O wretched man that I am! Who will deliver me from this body of death (Romans 7:18-19, 24)?

One of the surest indications that an individual is suffering from an addiction (e.g., alcohol, cocaine, nicotine, or porn) is their inability to stop using their "drug" of choice, even when aware of the negative impact it is having on their life.

Not to make light of other addictions, but for the genuinely born-again believer, a porn/sex addiction can be particularly agonizing. Longing with all his heart to be clean, but unable to find a way of escape from his habit (Romans 7:18-19), the under-siege Christian is especially prone to experiencing feelings of deep despair (Romans 7:24). Emotions can range from shame, to feelings of inadequacy as a husband and father, to fears of never one day hearing the words, "Well done, thou good and faithful servant (Matthew 25:21)." Some may even begin to question their salvation. Quite the agonizing place to be for the genuinely born-again believer. But it is here that he is condemned to stay, so long as he remains trapped in sexual sin.

Understanding how God designed the brain is key to breaking and staying free. This chapter explores the neurology of addiction, particularly those of a sexual nature. The addict's brain is defective and in need of repair. Subsequent chapters will therefore describe practical, Bible-based methods for reprogramming the brain by a renewing of the mind, through the transforming ministry of the Holy Spirit (Romans 12:2).

THE PLASTIC BRAIN

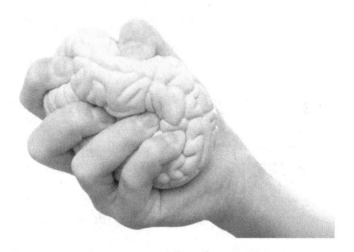

For centuries, the medical and scientific communities had assumed that the brain's anatomy was fixed. Conventional wisdom held that, after childhood, the brain changed only when it began the long process of decline.[1]

But much has changed in the last several decades. We now understand that the brain makes new connections, giving birth to new neurons with each new thought or action. Cradle-to-grave, for better or for worse, the brain is constantly changing and remolding itself. Each new thought or activity creates neural pathways that change the structure of the brain. Each time the thought or activity is repeated, the pathway deepens. For good or for bad, if repeated often enough, these pathways become subconsciously programmed into the mind.

Cradle-to-grave, for better or for worse, the brain is constantly changing and remolding itself.

Over time, these behavior-beaten pathways strengthen and begin firing automatically, with little or no conscious thought. This explains why an administrative assistant can increase from 50 to 100 words per minute after just several weeks on the job. Or why a golfer's handicap drops more rapidly once he begins going to a driving range between competitive rounds. Unfortunately, this same behavior-beaten pathway analogy also applies to the viewer of pornography.

THIS IS YOUR BRAIN ON PORN

Readers 40-and-older may recall the Partnership for a Drug-Free America's (PDFA) 1987 *This is Your Brain on Drugs* anti-narcotics campaign.[2] This public service announcement featured a spokesperson who opened by asking whether there is anyone who still did not understand the dangers of drug abuse. Holding up an egg, he goes on to say, "This is your brain." Motioning to a frying pan, he continues, "This is drugs." With the cracked egg frying in the pan, he adds, "This is your brain on drugs." Finally, he asks, "Any questions?" Thanks to advances in brain science, another image and tag line could now be tacked on to the PDFA's announcement. Motioning to an egg frying in a second pan, the spokesperson might now add, "This is your brain on porn."

Science has come a long way in the last 30-plus years. Imaging technology now allows us to clearly see both the drug-and-porn-inflicted damage to the brain that eggs and frying pans could only simplistically represent. Brain scans reveal clear similarities between a cocaine addict's brain and a porn addict's brain.[3] Both show damage and reduced blood flow to the prefrontal cortex, visual proof that the brain's chief command and impulse control center has been compromised. The scientific evidence is clear: Repeated viewing of pornography physically alters (damages) the structure of the brain.

Brain scans reveal clear similarities between a cocaine addict's brain and a porn addict's brain.[3]

THE CHEMICAL BRAIN

While sexual addiction almost always begins as a moral problem, imaging technology confirms that it ends up being very much a brain problem. The neurochemicals involved are out of balance, and the physical structure of the brain has been changed.

> **Dopamine**: A neurochemical responsible for experiencing reward and pleasure. God's design was for top-down (beginning in the prefrontal cortex) activation of these reward/pleasure circuits, as when: (i) having sex within the marriage covenant, (ii) passing the state Bar Exam on a first attempt, or (iii) hitting a walk-off homerun to win the state baseball championship.

> **Oxytocin & Vasopressin**: Bonding hormones that, among other things, promote monogamy in sexual relationships. In a marriage relationship, they bond a person to their partner during sexual release.

> **Endorphins (natural opioids)**: Chemically and functionally similar to opium and morphine, these neurochemicals reduce pain and enhance euphoria.

> **Testosterone**: The "male" hormone that drives sexual desire. Released naturally into the bloodstream throughout the day, levels increase in response to sexual signals from the brain.

At sexual release, these (and other) neurochemicals flood the brain, imparting to it the highest of chemical rewards. God designed us to produce these neurochemicals in healthy sexual relationships. But when a man regularly uses pornography to "act out" sexually, he sets himself up for bondage. Instead of neurologically bonding to his wife, he bonds to the images he is viewing. With continued use, the unhealthy porn pleasure pathways strengthen, while the God-designed pleasure pathways weaken. A chemical imbalance develops, causing the brain to depend increasingly on porn for pleasure and sexual release. Unaware that his reward circuitry is being hijacked, the "recreational" viewer of pornography is on a fast track to becoming a porn addict.

REASONING vs. EMOTIONAL BRAIN

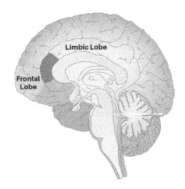

Median Section of the Human Brain

The Reasoning Brain: The prefrontal cortex, the brain's chief command and control center, is where higher reasoning takes place. It also functions as the brain's braking system, as this is the area of the brain responsible for discipline, postponing gratification, and controlling impulses.

The Emotional Brain: The limbic system is a central core area of the brain primarily responsible for processing emotions, and our survival, sexual, and aggressive instincts.[4] Among its many varied functions, we know that the limbic system is also involved in experiencing pleasure, and the formation of memories to repeat pleasure (e.g., it remembers that its owner dislikes veggies, likes pizza, and really likes porn). It is the gas pedal to the prefrontal cortex's braking system. This is the part of the brain where addiction takes place. Food, water, and sex are at the top of our God-designed reward list. These are natural rewards, as opposed to addictive substances (e.g., drugs, alcohol, and nicotine) and addictive behaviors (e.g., gambling, shopping, and viewing pornography), which can hijack our reward circuitry. Flooded with pleasurable neuro-chemicals, the brain is little concerned with whether its owner is feasting on pizza or porn; it just knows that "dopamine is good."[5] For better or for worse, the brain creates emotional attachments that lock these pleasurable experiences into long-term memory. Repeated often enough, its owner sets himself up for bondage as he neurochemically attaches to these experiences.

Just as the sound of a bell caused Pavlov's dogs to salivate, even little things associated with a pleasurable experience can kick off cravings. The junkie sees a needle and begins craving his next fix. For the porn addict, the rush may come at the sight of a particularly striking woman, when driving by an adult video store, or knowing that he is going to be home alone with an unprotected computer later that evening.

NOVELTY, TOLERANCE, AND ESCALATION

The brain loves novelty. Be it a candy bar, or a pornographic video, when it experiences something new and pleasurable, it releases a surge of dopamine to strengthen that behavioral circuit. It also stores a "feels good" imprint in memory to make it easy to repeat the pleasurable activity. But with repeated use, the activity's novelty wears thin, and the brain develops a tolerance. What used to excite no longer does the trick, and dopamine levels begin to fall off. No problem for the chocolate lover; he simply moves on to another brand of candy bar. But this is where things really begin to get scary for the viewer of pornography.

With dopamine levels falling off, the brain now requires increasingly novel and/or hardcore forms of pornography to achieve the same sexual high.[6,7,8] And what better medium to deliver these increasingly novel/hardcore forms of pornography than today's high-speed Internet?

It used to be that trips to the downtown adult bookstore were limited by the time and effort involved, the money required, and the risk of being seen. But these were still only static images, with limited novelty. Not the stuff of today's HD-videos-gone-wild Internet porn, with its addictive power.

Premium cable channels arrived next on the scene. Movies replaced the magazine's static images. Gone also was the risk of being seen in the bookstore parking lot or at the check-out counter. But, initially at least, cable porn was limited in novelty to only a few standard genres. And it still wasn't cheap.

Fast-forward to today, and the "three *A*s of the Internet." [9] With only a few keystrokes and mouse clicks (Accessibility), websites featuring high-definition video clips of any type of sexual behavior may be freely accessed (Affordability) in the privacy of one's own home (Anonymity). And when the brain begins to develop a tolerance, other more novel/hardcore websites—with constantly updated content—are always just a few more clicks away. Someone who began as a "recreational" viewer of the naked female form must now access websites featuring these increasingly novel/hardcore forms of pornography to achieve the same sexual high.

The brain's love of novelty and the high-speed Internet (with its seemingly inexhaustible supply of novelty) have combined to create the scariest of perfect storms. At least the nicotine addict has the Surgeon General's warning label stamped on every pack of cigarettes. But there are no warning labels for the viewer of pornography. Unaware that their reward circuitry is being hijacked, those that continue to dabble in porn are unknowingly setting themselves up for bondage. And the situation is only likely to worsen with the Internet now accessible, via smartphones, by individuals of all ages worldwide.

HOPE FOR HEALING

And do not be conformed to this world, but be transformed by the renewing of your mind, that you may prove what is that good and acceptable and perfect will of God (Romans 12:2).

As desperate as the porn/sex addict's case might seem, all is not lost. As described in the Bible nearly 2000 years ago, it is possible to reverse the damage and have the mind renewed through the transforming ministry of the Holy Spirit (Romans 12:2). Because God designed our brains to be plastic until death, there is always hope for healing. Science now confirms this biblical truth. With the discovery of neuroplasticity, the scientific community now also understands that it is possible to physically restructure the brain.

> *Neuroscience now confirms what Scripture has been saying for nearly 2000 years—it is possible to physically restructure the brain by renewing it spiritually through the transforming ministry of the Holy Spirit.*

REPROGRAMMING THE BRAIN

The limbic system is the brain's seat of emotions and an input receiver for the senses (think emotional, visual). Imprints of the images the porn addict has viewed are also stored in memory in the limbic system. It is here therefore, in the limbic system, that most of the battle

39

for the brain takes place. For healing to occur, the limbic system must be accessed and the brain reprogrammed. [10,11]

> ### *For healing to occur, the limbic system must be accessed and the brain reprogrammed. [10,11]*

When the flesh mounts a sensual (strongly emotional), image-laden (strongly visual) attack and the addict's counterattack is a words-only prayer or memory verse (lightly emotional, non-visual), the result is predictably bad. Why? Because, at best, the latter only lightly engages the brain's limbic system. But if the counterattack combines words with spiritually-and-emotionally-charged imagery, the brain is engaged in a much more powerful way, and the flesh can be repelled.

In the *Way of Escape* Battle Plan, the limbic system is accessed with highly emotional and highly visual content each time one of the Spirit-anointed apps is viewed (see *My Library of 23 Spirit-Anointed, Flesh-Diffusing Applications*, Chapter 7). With each viewing, new and healthier neural pathways are created. With each repeated viewing, these pathways deepen. Over time, these healthier, Spirit-anointed neural pathways become the new second nature, firing with little or no conscious thought, while the unhealthy, now-idle fleshly pathways are pruned back (according to the promise of Galatians 5:16, see Chapter 6). With each viewing of the Spirit-anointed, flesh-diffusing apps, the mind is being renewed, and the brain is being transformed (Romans 12:2).

> ### *With each viewing of the Spirit-anointed, flesh-diffusing apps, the mind is being renewed, and the brain is being transformed (Romans 12:2).*

The steps required to build a library of Spirit-anointed, flesh-diffusing apps are described in Chapters 6-7. But first, in Chapters 3-5, we examine three pre-emptive strike options for attacking the flesh while it is yet in a relatively weakened state.

3

IDENTIFY AND EXERCISE SPIRITUAL GIFTS

But the manifestation of the Spirit is given to *each one* for the profit of all: For to one is given the word of wisdom through the Spirit, to another the word of knowledge through the same Spirit, To another faith by the same Spirit, to another gifts of healing by the same Spirit, To another the working of miracles, to another prophecy, to another discerning of spirits, to another different kinds of tongues, to another the interpretation of tongues. But one and the same Spirit works all these things, distributing to *each one* individually as He wills (I Corinthians 12:7-11).

God has equipped *each* born-again believer (I Corinthians 12:7a, 12:11b) with at least one spiritual gift, to glorify God (I Peter 4:11), and to edify the Church (I Corinthians 12:7b, Ephesians 4:12c). How critical that one discovers his spiritual gift(s), for they determine the believer's function and purpose in the Body of Christ.[1]

How critical that one discovers his spiritual gift(s), for they determine the believer's function and

41

purpose in the Body of Christ.[1]

Without receiving instruction on spiritual gifts, some will still naturally develop ministries that utilize their gifts in an effective manner. But others, unaware that they even possess spiritual gifts, will rarely exercise them and, sadly, fall far short of realizing their full potential as a Christian.

More alarming than wasting one's gift(s) is the resulting idle time, with its attendant temptations. The devil must flee all who submit and draw nigh unto God (James 4:7-8a). But a profession of faith, empty of follow-on good works, leaves the too-much-time-on-his-hands believer much more vulnerable to attacks of the flesh. More than not realizing his full potential as a Christian, the less-than-vigilant believer opens himself up to the devil's attacks (I Peter 5:8). But this need not be his continuing state. He can reduce the number of enemy "incomings" by simply identifying his spiritual gifts and then filling his idle, temptation-filled days with ministries that exercise these gifts.

SPIRITUAL GIFTS

God has equipped each born-again believer with at least one spiritual gift (I Corinthians 12:7a, 12:11b). A cursory review of online websites found lists containing up to 25 different Bible-based spiritual gifts. C. Peter Wagner, the international bestselling author, who for the last three decades has been a leading voice for spiritual gifts and the "priesthood of all believers" (I Peter 2:9), sets the number at 28.[2]

Most lists include a core group of 20, cited in the three primary passages on spiritual gifts—I Corinthians 12:1-31, Romans 12:4-8, and Ephesians 4:11-13. Those gifts over-and-above the core 20 (e.g., hospitality, intercession) are taken from Scripture passages that are only tangentially discussing spiritual gifts. In what follows, only the 20 core gifts from the three primary passages on spiritual gifts are listed, along with Wagner's brief definition of each.

1. **Administration (I Corinthians 12:28)** – To understand clearly the immediate and long-term goals of a particular group within the Body of Christ, and to devise/execute effective plans for the accomplishment of those goals.

2. **Apostle (I Corinthians 12:28, Ephesians 4:11)** – To assume and to exercise divinely imparted authority to establish the foundational government of an assigned sphere of ministry within the Church.

3. **Discernment (I Corinthians 12:10)** – To know with assurance that certain behaviors purported to be of God are in reality divine (vs. human or satanic).

4. **Evangelism (Ephesians 4:11)** – To share the gospel with unbelievers in such a way that men and women become Jesus' disciples and responsible members of the Body of Christ.

5. **Exhortation (Romans 12:8)** – To minister words of comfort, consolation, encouragement, and counsel to other members of the Body of Christ in such a way that they are helped or healed.

6. **Faith (I Corinthians 12:9)** – To discern with extraordinary confidence the will and purposes of God for the future of His work.

7. **Giving (Romans 12:8)** – To contribute their material resources to the work of the Lord liberally and cheerfully, above and beyond the tithes and offerings expected of all believers.

8. **Healing (I Corinthians 12:9, 12:28)** – To serve as human intermediaries through whom God chooses to cure illness and restore health, apart from natural means.

9. **Helps (I Corinthians 12:28)** – To invest the talents they have in the life and ministry of other members of the Body of Christ, thus enabling those others to increase the effectiveness of their own spiritual gifts.

10. **Interpretation of Tongues (I Corinthians 12:10, 12:30)** – To make known in the vernacular the message of one who

speaks in tongues.

11. **Knowledge (I Corinthians 12:8)** – To discover, accumulate, analyze, and clarify information and ideas which are pertinent to the growth and well-being of the Body of Christ.

12. **Leadership (Romans 12:8)** – To set goals in accordance with God's purpose, and to communicate these goals to others in such a way that they voluntarily and harmoniously work together to accomplish those goals for the glory of God.

13. **Mercy (Romans 12:8)** – To feel genuine empathy and compassion for individuals, both Christian and non-Christian, who suffer distressing physical, mental, or emotional problems, and to translate that compassion into cheerfully done deeds that reflect Christ's love, and alleviate the suffering.

14. **Miracles (I Corinthians 12:10, 12:28)** – To serve as human intermediaries through whom God chooses to perform powerful acts that are perceived by observers to have altered the ordinary course of nature.

15. **Pastor (Ephesians 4:11)** – To assume a long-term personal responsibility for the spiritual welfare of a group of believers.

16. **Prophecy (I Corinthians 12:10, 12:28, Romans 12:6, Ephesians 4:11)** – To receive and communicate an immediate message of God to His people through a divinely anointed utterance.

17. **Service (Romans 12:7)** – To identify the unmet needs involved in a task related to God's work, and to make use of available resources to meet those needs and help accomplish the desired goals.

18. **Teaching (I Corinthians 12:28, Romans 12:7, Ephesians 4:11)** – To communicate information relevant to the health and ministry of the Body of Christ in such a way that others will learn.

19. **Tongues (I Corinthians 12:10, 12:30)** – To: (i) speak to God in a language they have never learned, and/or (ii) receive and communicate an immediate message from God to His people through a divinely anointed utterance in a language they have never learned.

20. **Wisdom (I Corinthians 12:8)** – To know the mind of the Holy Spirit in such a way as to receive insight into how given knowledge may best be applied to specific needs arising in the Body of Christ.

SPIRITUAL GIFTS TESTS

I am still in possession of results from two spiritual gifts tests that I had taken back in 2000 and 2002. In the first, knowledge, teaching, and helps ranked the highest. In the second, it was teaching again, followed by evangelism and mercy. These results were fairly consistent with each other and with ministries undertaken within the Church to that point in my Christian walk. Since being saved in 1989, I had regularly acquired *knowledge* that might be used in *teaching* classes on Christian apologetics that would ultimately point the lost to Christ (*evangelism*).

As I contemplated writing this book, I thought that it might be instructive to test my spiritual gifts again. Have my gifts changed in the last 15-plus years, or have they remained substantially the same?

A third spiritual gifts test was taken online in July 2017.[3] Teaching and evangelism were my two highest-ranking gifts, followed by faith. These results were not at all surprising, given that, exercising my gifts as a teacher, I had recently published a highly evangelistic book—*100 Reasons to Believe the Bible is the Word of God*.[4]

In February 2018, I took the spiritual gifts test in the back of Wagner's book.[5] This time there was a three-way tie at the top between teaching, knowledge, and evangelism. These results were also quite consistent with earlier test results dating back to 2000.

A "Spiritual Gifts Scorecard" is constructed from the four tests taken in the last two decades (see table, to follow). Six (6) points are awarded for each test; three (3) to the most dominant gift, two (2) to the runner-up, and one (1) to the third-place finisher. The three-way tie in the fourth test results in each of the three top scoring gifts receiving an equal portion of the six (6) total points awarded.

While no man-made test can perfectly measure the spiritual, it does seem safe to conclude that teaching is my dominant gift. That my primary ministries in the Church to date have been in the areas of teaching and writing seems to validate the test results, as do my final 17 years in the workplace, employed as a college instructor.

Spiritual Gifts Scorecard

SPIRITUAL GIFT	TEST #1 (2000)	TEST #2 (2002)	TEST #3 (2017)	TEST #4 (2018)	TOTAL
Evangelism	---	2	2	2	6
Faith	---	---	1	---	1
Helps	1	---	---	---	1
Knowledge	3	---	---	2	5
Mercy	---	1	---	---	1
Teaching	2	3	3	2	10

EXERCISING MY SPIRITUAL GIFTS

The consistency of test results, along with validation from both within and without the Church, suggests that I should continue along this same trajectory. Now retired, I am no longer positioned to exercise my gift of teaching as a college instructor. But within the Body of Christ, these gifts can easily find expression: (i) in the local church teaching Sunday School Class electives, and (ii) in the Universal Church writing books that focus on Christian apologetics, evangelism, and gaining a better knowledge/understanding of the Bible and its teachings.

Dear reader, if you have yet to discover your spiritual gift(s), I encourage you to begin by going through a process similar to that described in this chapter. Wagner's book is an excellent resource. There are also numerous websites offering free tests to help you identify your spiritual gift(s) and calling. Once identified, you can then plug into those specific roles in the Body of Christ (and the workplace) that are best suited to your gifts.

As you work through the process of identifying and exercising your spiritual gifts, I further encourage you to keep a record of the number of attacks of the flesh. You should experience a noticeable reduction in the number of enemy "incomings" as you begin to fill your once-idle, temptation-filled days with ministries that exercise your spiritual gifts.

JANUARY 2022 UPDATE: Save for the section to follow, this entire chapter was written in early 2018. Over the next four years, I would come to better know the mind of the Holy Spirit. Sure enough, upon retaking Wagner's spiritual gifts test (TEST #4) in January of 2022, I found that wisdom was now my highest-ranking spiritual gift (gift #20 in the list of 20, two pages prior). Gifts can change and should be periodically re-tested.

THE *WAY OF ESCAPE* BATTLE PLAN: NO SPECIAL SPIRITUAL GIFTS REQUIRED

(Please note that the author does *not* possess the gift of tongues)

With "Spirit-Powered" appearing in the title of the book and "Holy Spirit dove" images leading off each chapter, two questions have perhaps come to the reader's mind.

Who Can Realize the Full Spiritual Benefits of the *Way of Escape* Battle Plan? The Holy Spirit can deliver only those in whom He dwells (John 14:17). I can overcome the flesh by walking in the Spirit (Galatians 5:16) only if I have first been born of the Spirit (John 3:3-8). The full spiritual benefits of the *Way of Escape* Battle Plan may therefore only be realized by those who have first been born of the Spirit.

Are Any Special Spiritual Gifts Required? No. All who have been born of the Spirit have been empowered to walk in the Spirit. Most, however, only do so to some very limited degree. The still-struggling may simply need to learn how to step up the degree to which they are walking in the Spirit (see *The Galatians 5:16 Revelation*, Chapter 6). The still-struggling may simply need to drop the passivity, and learn how to actively pursue more regular relationship intimacy with the Holy Spirit (see KEY REGULARITY, Chapter 6).

All who have been born of the Spirit may realize the full spiritual benefits of the *Way of Escape* Battle Plan. No special spiritual gifts are required.

THE OFFENDING EYE REMOVED

"If your right eye causes you to sin, pluck it out and cast it from you; for it is more profitable for you that one of your members perish, than for your whole body to be cast into hell (Matthew 5:29)."

This verse of Scripture is certainly not to be taken literally. For even if I were to pluck out the right eye, the equally offensive left eye would remain. Properly interpreted, this chapter's focus verse is saying that I am to exercise extreme caution concerning those things that I allow to pass before my eyes.

All materials that are pornographic in nature must go. Any electronic devices that bring these offensive materials before my eyes must also either go (preferred) or be effectively neutralized. I cannot win this battle if I am unwilling to let go of the devices that the enemy (the flesh) is using to trip me up.

ELECTRONIC DEVICES IN THE HOME

Laptop: Most Christian authors and sexual purity programs recommend installing accountability/blocking software on all electronic devices that are Internet-connected. I went one step further. I chose to be without the Internet in my home. Except for the first eight months that I owned a smartphone (June 2016 to February 2017, see the sub-section to follow), the last time that I accessed the Internet from my home was in January of 2010. Now whenever I absolutely need to go online, I access the Internet through my local library or at local eateries that offer free wi-fi. In this age of high technology (and high temptation), I am happy to say that, in my home, my laptop is not much more than a glorified typewriter.

Smartphone: I arrived late on the smartphone scene. I did not upgrade to a smartphone until I lost my flip phone in the Gulf of Mexico in June of 2016. Initially, my plan called for 0.50 GB of cell data each month. But after seeing the temptation that it provided, even that was eliminated (February 2017). Today, my plan provides me with exactly *zero* GB of cell data each month. More robust plans are certainly available, but once more, I have made the conscious decision to be without the Internet in my home. I can, of course, still use my smartphone to access the Internet through any one of a number of public wi-fi hotspots. But in my home, I am happy to say that my "smartphone" is nothing more than a phone with texting capability.

Cable TV: I have never allowed either hardcore or softcore pornographic cable channels into my home. Countless hours have, however, been wasted watching cable TV. Desiring to be free of the distractions and milder forms of temptation it provides, I dropped standard cable in December of 2012.

> *No Internet on my laptop. Zero GB of cell data on my smartphone. No cable TV. Let each reader tailor their Battle Plan to fit their unique situation.*

DVD Players: The only remaining electronic devices in my home that are capable of being used to view pornographic material are a 9-inch DVD player equipped with a built-in display monitor and two other DVD players connected to 32-and-50-inch television monitors. These devices are, however, now only used to view things (e.g., workout DVDs) that are pure and of good report (Philippians 4:8). They also turned out to be indispensable research tools while writing this book. As described more fully in Chapters 6-7, they were used to screen candidates under consideration for inclusion in my library of Spirit-anointed, flesh-diffusing apps.

While these recommended practices worked well for me, they may be too extreme—or even impractical—for others. For example, it may not be feasible for some to be without the Internet in the home. For these persons, an accountability/blocking software program such as *CovenantEyes*[1] should be installed on all computers and phones. Each reader will have to tailor their Battle Plan to fit their unique situation (see *Appendix A* for additional options).

SPRING 2020 UPDATE: The preceding section of text was written in early 2018. When the COVID-19 pandemic closed local libraries and eateries in March 2020, I lost my safe access to the Internet. But I still required Internet access to build an online following for the book. For the first time in over a decade, the Internet was grudgingly back in my home. But without incident. The Spirit-anointed apps had long since rewired neural pathways.

ELECTRONIC DEVICES IN THE OFFICE

For those employed in an office environment, a few commonsense safeguards can go a long way towards keeping even an unprotected work computer from becoming a stumbling block.

> *A few commonsense safeguards can go a long way towards keeping even an unprotected work computer from becoming a stumbling block.*

Hallway-Facing Monitor: Locate the computer such that the monitor is always visible from the hallway. Foot traffic, particularly down a carpeted hallway, is a terrific accountability partner.

See-Through Windows: If colleagues are adding privacy film to their office windows, resist the temptation to follow their lead. See-through office windows are another terrific accountability partner. A little lost privacy is a small price to pay to maintain one's sexual integrity in the workplace.

Spirit-Anointed, Flesh-Diffusing Apps Folder: As your library of Spirit-anointed, flesh-diffusing apps begins to take shape (you will learn how to construct this library in Chapter 7), add a folder with links to these apps to your computer's desktop. So long as it does not interfere with your work, have these apps softly playing, pre-emptively, in the background. This will aid in both heading off attacks of the flesh and in healing. With each pass through your expanding playlist, new and healthier neural pathways are created, and existing ones are deepened.

Never Alone: Avoid situations and times that leave you alone in the office. If you do find yourself alone, move to a community computer lab where others can serve as unsuspecting accountability partners. If this is not an option at your workplace, and you absolutely must remain alone in the office, have a playlist of your Spirit-anointed, flesh-diffusing apps playing continuously in the background to head off attacks of the flesh.

These few commonsense safeguards can go a long way towards keeping even an unprotected work computer from becoming a stumbling block. If the flesh is still occasionally breaking through, accountability/ blocking software should be installed. Each reader will have to tailor their Battle Plan to fit their unique situation (see *Appendix A* for additional options).

ELECTRONIC DEVICES IN THE HOTEL ROOM

For those struggling with a porn/sex addiction, I suspect that the hotel room will be one of the more difficult places to maintain sexual integrity. It is therefore recommended that solo stays in hotel rooms be avoided whenever possible, and particularly in the initial stages of recovery.

Recall that I chose to be without the Internet in my home. So long as I am in the home, there is therefore no need to have accountability/ blocking software installed on any of my electronic devices. But that all changes when I spend a night alone in a hotel room offering free access to the Internet. To head off this temptation, I must either: (i) have my electronic devices protected by an accountability/blocking software program, or (ii) leave my electronic devices at home. Don't laugh! If maintaining sexual integrity while traveling is important to you, it may well be possible to develop a workable plan around a modified form of that second option.

Laptop: If I am traveling alone, my laptop stays at home. Many hotels now provide access to the Internet with community computers, usually located just off the main lobby area. It requires making a few extra phone calls before hitting the road, but I will only stay at hotels that provide this service. If I need to be online for a more extended time, the local public library is also always an option. These little inconveniences are a small price for me, an infrequent traveler, to pay to maintain my sexual integrity. For the more frequent traveler, having accountability/ blocking software installed on their electronic devices is a better option. Each reader will have to tailor their Battle Plan to fit their unique situation (see *Appendix A* for additional options).

Smartphone: When I must stay alone in a hotel while traveling, the room is off-limits to my smartphone. I make sure that all phone-related tasks are completed outside of the hotel room, in public, during normal daytime working hours. When it's time to head to the room at the end of the day, the smartphone stays locked in my car's glove compartment. Again, another small price to pay to maintain my sexual integrity when traveling alone.

While this practice works well for me, individuals still in the initial stages of recovery will not yet possess the discipline necessary to leave their smartphone in the car overnight. For these individuals, having accountability/blocking software installed on their electronic devices is a better option. Each reader will have to tailor their Battle Plan to fit their unique situation (see *Appendix A* for additional options).

Cable TV: When traveling alone, I will only stay in hotels that agree to either disable my cable connection or physically remove the television from my room. This again requires making a few extra phone calls before hitting the road. But it is well worth the extra effort to maintain my sexual integrity while traveling.

DVD Player: A book bag has always been a part of my luggage when traveling. It would contain my Bible, other current reads, and healthy snacks. To these, I have now added my 9-inch DVD player with built-in display monitor and those Homecoming concert DVDs containing my most powerful Spirit-anointed apps (see *My Library of 23 Spirit-Anointed, Flesh-Diffusing Applications*, Chapter 7). These DVDs are now my in-room viewing entertainment. Played in pre-emptive mode, they severely constrain the flesh's ability to launch an attack. And for those rare occasions when the flesh might still manage to break through, my most powerful Spirit-anointed apps are all only a "Play" away, standing at the ready to be launched in counterattack mode.

No laptop. No hotel room access for my smartphone. No cable TV. A DVD player and DVDs featuring my most powerful Spirit-anointed apps included in my luggage. Let each reader tailor their Battle Plan when traveling to fit their unique situation.

SPRING 2020 UPDATE: The preceding section of text was written in early 2018. A good set of recommended practices for the hotel room for the individual still in the initial stages of recovery. But once the Spirit-anointed apps rewire neural pathways, most of these practices may be relaxed. Each reader will have to tailor their Battle Plan to fit their unique situation.

WATCH AND PRAY

"Watch and pray, lest you enter into temptation. The spirit indeed is willing, but the flesh is weak (Matthew 26:41)."

When I came to saving faith in Christ, I entered a heated battle. Like it or not, my profession of faith enlisted me as one of God's soldiers in a battle between the flesh and the Spirit. Three passages of Scripture that give glimpses into this battle have already been referenced (Romans 7:17-25, Galatians 5:17, Matthew 5:29). The focus verse of this chapter (Matthew 26:41) provides a fourth.

This talk of battles between the flesh and Spirit may be a little overwhelming for the person with a porn/sex addiction. But take heart, dear reader. This chapter's focus verse includes an implied promise of "temptation avoidance" for all who commit to *pre-emptively* watch and pray (Matthew 26:41a). There is much that can be done in the way of "watching and praying" to prevent the flesh from launching many of its attacks.

There is much that can be done in the way of "watching and praying" to prevent the flesh from launching many of its attacks.

DROP THE PASSIVITY

The first half of Matthew 26:41 is a call to action. If sexual purity is the goal, then I must drop the passivity. Instead of passively waiting for the flesh to launch an attack, I must go on the offensive to head off these attacks by watching and praying:

- **Avoid Predictable Attacks (Watching, Part I)**: I must make a conscious effort to avoid predictable attacks of the flesh that have caused me to stumble in the past
- **Diffuse Surprise Attacks (Watching, Part II)**: I must launch pre-emptive strikes to tap into the Holy Spirit's power to diffuse surprise attacks of the flesh
- **Targeted Prayer**: I must offer up Scripture-based prayers that specifically promise "temptation avoidance" and escape from temptation

AVOID PREDICTABLE ATTACKS

Experience teaches that there are certain more predictable times when the flesh might even be *expected* to launch an attack. Weekend evenings are a time of heightened temptation for many. Though far from perfect accountability partners, busy work schedules tend to keep the flesh more at bay from Sunday evening through Friday afternoon. If the flesh is to strike, it might predictably do so when discretionary time and times of idleness peak on the weekends. It is for these more predictable times of heightened temptation that I must be especially careful to "watch" that I might not be caught with my guard down.

I know my times of heightened temptation. And it is at these times that I have historically stumbled the most often. If I am serious about living sexually pure, then, at a first and most fundamental level of "watching," I must make a conscious effort to avoid those situations and places that have caused me to stumble in the past. It does little good for the recovering alcoholic to pray that he remains sober and then spend the rest of the evening in his favorite bar. In like manner, it does little good for the recovering porn addict to pray that he enters not into temptation and then spend the rest of the evening home alone, surfing the Internet on an unprotected computer.

At a first and most fundamental level of "watching,"
I must make a conscious effort to avoid those
situations and places that have caused me to
stumble in the past.

Here, it was assumed that weekend evenings would be the times of highest vulnerability to attacks of the flesh. For those with non-standard schedules, other times may pose more of a threat. Each reader will have to tailor their Battle Plan to their unique situation.

DIFFUSE SURPRISE ATTACKS

While some attacks of the flesh are predictable, many are not. Much to the addict's dismay, attacks of the flesh can often come out of nowhere, brought on by any of a number of triggering events. For the person with a porn/sex addiction, avoiding even the most predictable attacks of the flesh is a challenge. Having to now fend off all its "surprise" attacks can lead to feelings of despair and thoughts of giving up.

But the situation is not nearly as hopeless as it might first appear. In one of the more pleasant surprises of this work, I found that even most "surprise" attacks can be eliminated by regular, near-daily viewing of the Spirit-anointed apps (see Chapter 7) *in pre-emptive mode*, while the flesh is yet in a relatively weakened state. I had been practicing various forms of the Chapter 3-5 spiritual disciplines my entire Christian life. While these disciplines were essential for spiritual growth, they still left me facing an estimated 10 attacks of the flesh per month (see *Real Data*, Chapter 8). But after I began regular, near-daily viewing/screening of the Spirit-anointed, flesh-diffusing apps, enemy "incomings" fell to approximately two (2) much more easily diffused attacks per month (again, see *Real Data*, Chapter 8).

Even most "surprise" attacks can be eliminated by regular, near-daily viewing of the Spirit-anointed apps in pre-emptive mode, while the flesh is yet in a relatively weakened state.

TARGETED PRAYER

Scripture teaches (Matthew 26:41, James 1:14-15)—and experience confirms—that once temptation is entertained, a subsequent fall into sin is almost certain. Advances in neuroscience help to explain why. From a favorite food to a forbidden fruit, once a pleasurable activity is anticipated, dopamine (the "pleasure molecule") floods the brain's reward circuitry, making it nearly impossible to turn back (see *Reasoning vs. Emotional Brain*, Chapter 2). This pleasure craving is especially powerful when tempted sexually, as sexual stimulation and release add up to the biggest natural dose of dopamine available to the brain's reward circuitry.[1]

With sin nearly always following so closely on the heels of temptation, it is understandable why Jesus does not say "watch and pray to *defeat* temptation," but rather "watch and pray to *avoid* temptation" (Matthew 26:41a). There will still be casualties in even the most successfully waged battle. But there will be zero casualties in a battle that never takes place. I must always be watching and praying for ways to *avoid* temptation.

Jesus does not say "watch and pray to defeat temptation," but rather "watch and pray to avoid temptation" (Matthew 26:41a).

Appendix B gathers together key Scripture passages that deal with both "temptation avoidance" and escaping temptation. Passages describing the Holy Spirit's role in engineering the escape are also included. The embedded promises are extracted, tailored specifically to sexual temptations, and then collectively claimed in *A Prayer for Sexual Purity.*

A RENEWED MIND

I cannot overstate the importance of removing the Internet from the home. Dropping cable is also highly recommended. I found that removing just these two temptations (and continuing to practice the Chapter 3-5 spiritual disciplines) while also regularly viewing the Spirit-anointed apps (see Chapter 7) *in pre-emptive mode* eliminated nearly all attacks of the flesh (see *Real Data*, Chapter 8). Perhaps this shouldn't be so surprising. Nearly 2000 years ago, God's Word stated that such a renewing of the mind was not only possible, but that it was the reasonable expectation for all who have been born of the Spirit (Romans 12:2):

> *And do not be conformed to this world, but be transformed by the renewing of your mind, that you may prove what is that good and acceptable and perfect will of God (Romans 12:2).*

WALKING IN THE SPIRIT

I say then: Walk in the Spirit, and you shall not fulfill the lust of the flesh (Galatians 5:16).

Christian leaders and commentators have long encouraged fellow believers to heed the admonitions of Scripture (e.g., plug into ministry, remove the offending eye, watch and pray) in their battle to overcome the flesh. The basic content of Chapters 3-5 is, therefore, not new. It simply echoes these oft-preached messages, modified, of course, for the new forms that temptation has assumed in the Internet Age. In this chapter, we take a fresh look at the Holy Spirit, and His central role in delivering believers from fleshly lusts (Galatians 5:16).

A BATTLE RAGES

Pre-conversion, the Spirit can only convict of sin. The flesh, however, is already hard at work, enticing with many "harmless" activities such as masturbation, watching porn, and frequenting strip bars. For some, the "harmless" activities may escalate to morally reprehensible—but still legal—acts, such as cheating on a girlfriend or spouse. Left unchecked, offenses that are deemed inappropriate or illegal, even by today's loose societal standards, may follow (e.g., sexual harassment, indecent exposure, and solicitation).

At conversion, a different dynamic begins to play out. Indwelt by the Holy Spirit, the "harmless" activities are now seen for what they truly are—sins against a Holy God (Job 31:1, Matthew 5:28). The genuinely born-again believer would have all these tendencies to sin forever removed. But the old man, with all his pre-conversion baggage, will not go quietly. Thus begins, in every born-again believer, a battle between the flesh and the Spirit (Galatians 5:17).

God is the Author of our sexuality. In the proper setting, sex is one of life's most beautiful experiences. But what does the born-again believer do when the flesh makes an unwanted house call? When the flesh does come calling, too many men, even in the Church, will "act out" sexually. This is a big problem. Men trapped in sexual sins will not be able to lead, and the Church is suffering tremendously as a result.

All Christian authors and purity programs that I have reviewed insist that this is a battle that cannot be won alone. If it is to be successful, an accountability partner/group must be part of any recovery program. In support of this position, Scripture passages encouraging the confession of sin to a fellow Christian are often cited (e.g., Galatians 6:1-2, James 5:16), as are the added benefits of building community and stronger churches.

Despite these strong and convincing arguments, I suspect that most Christian men will opt out of such programs once made aware that they must spill their sexual sins in a group setting (*most* is quantified in Appendix C). Even if this was the only available option, I suspect that most Christian men will still choose to hoist the white flag, acknowledge defeat, and resign themselves to a hypocritical, inconsistent walk, conceding that, "This is just a part of who I am, and I will never be able to completely shake this addiction." They may even cite passages like Romans 7:17-25 and Galatians 5:17 to wrongly justify their inconsistent walk.

But what if a Battle Plan could be developed that would allow the *individual* Christian—apart from an accountability group—to escape temptation, even in those moments when the flesh is banging down the door? This work proposes to offer just such a Battle Plan, with "walking in the Spirit" its key component and Spirit-anointed, limbic weaponry (think emotional, visual) the fast-acting catalyst of spiritual reaction.

In the Way of Escape *Battle Plan, "walking in the Spirit" is the key component and Spirit-anointed, limbic weaponry (think emotional, visual) the fast-acting catalyst of spiritual reaction.*

NOT IN THIS BATTLE ALONE

Praise God, we are not in this battle alone. The Holy Spirit resides within each genuinely born-again believer. And He is ready, willing, and more-than-able to provide a way of escape—and ultimate, lasting victory—for all who sincerely desire to overcome a porn/sex addiction.

> *The Holy Spirit resides within each genuinely born-again believer. And He is ready, willing, and more-than-able to provide a way of escape for all who sincerely desire to overcome a porn/sex addiction.*

Healing was a big part of Jesus' earthly ministry. It was by His works (including healing) that He showed Himself to be One with the Father (John 10:37-38). Jesus, of course, no longer walks this earth. But He has left a Helper and Comforter (John 16:7), the Holy Spirit, who continues to testify of Him (John 15:26). Today, it is to the Holy Spirit that believers should be looking for healing and deliverance from their addictions.

It is the Spirit that sets us free from the sins that we cannot get free of on our own (Romans 8:2-4). It is the Spirit that enables us to fulfill the righteous requirements of the law (Romans 8:4). Requirements that we could never have fulfilled on our own. For more on what three of America's most beloved pastors (Charles Stanley, Francis Chan, and John MacArthur) have to say on lingering sins and God's provision for eradicating them, see Appendix D.

> *For the law of the Spirit of life in Christ Jesus has made me free from the law of sin and death. For what the law could not do in that it was weak through the flesh, God did by sending His own Son ... That the righteous requirement of the law might be fulfilled in us who do not walk according to the flesh but according to the Spirit (Romans 8:2-4).*

THE GALATIANS 5:16 REVELATION

> ***KEY VERSE: I say then: Walk in the Spirit, and you shall not fulfill the lust of the flesh (Galatians 5:16).***

The year is 2017. Early Fall. Late September or early October. I don't recall the exact date. Since the 2017 July Fourth Weekend, I have been poring over Bible Commentaries, studying Scripture passages on the Holy Spirit.

How often I had read Galatians 5:16 and moved on, thinking to myself, "I've been born of the Spirit, so, of course, I am always walking in the Spirit." But Galatians 5:16 says that if I am walking in the Spirit, then I will not fulfill the lust of the flesh. And since coming to Christ in 1989, I had, on more than a few occasions, still chosen to fulfill the lust of the flesh. I'm walking in the Spirit (or so I thought), but still fulfilling the lust of the flesh? This ought not to be! What am I missing? [**Mid-Study Note to Self**: Of the Scripture passages I'm studying on the Holy Spirit, here's one that I need to revisit.]

Initially, this was a bitter pill to swallow, for I was now aware that I was not quite the sanctified Christian that I had always fancied myself to be. But despair would soon give way to gladness, as this verse also seemed to be suggesting a way of escape. Being a born-again, Spirit-indwelt child of God is a necessary condition for conquering the flesh. But I must also be walking in the Spirit. And apparently, to some degree/regularity exceeding my Fall 2017 walk.

OK. I needed to step up my game. But come on. Is it really possible in this porn/sex-crazed world to go any significant length of time and not fulfill the lust of the flesh? Perhaps a few Church leaders can live up to this standard. But does God really expect ordinary lay Christians to walk this victoriously? Hear what Bible Commentators are saying about Galatians 5:16, and this matter of walking in the Spirit:

> Paul is not talking to "super Christians" in this passage ... This is not a deeper life or higher life; this is the normal Christian life ... If we are submitting to the Spirit, we cannot gratify the flesh.[1]

> ... this does not mean that by the gift of the Spirit a

redeemed person escapes the need to struggle against sin. The Spirit simply makes the victory possible—and that only to the degree that the believer "lives by the Spirit" or "walks" in Him.[2]

… walk is used here in the present tense, indicating that Paul is speaking of continuous, regular action… a habitual way of life… The life walked by the Spirit is no different from being "filled with the Spirit" (Ephesians 5:18), a phrase referring to the controlling power exerted by the Spirit on a willing Christian.[3]

A key phrase above is "to the degree that the believer 'lives by the Spirit' or 'walks' in Him." Most believers have only a passive relationship with the Holy Spirit. They know Him, alright. They were fully indwelt by Him at conversion, of course. But only occasionally do they now experience relationship intimacy with Him. Something the pastor said in Sunday's sermon tugged on their heart. The week before it was the choir's rendition of a favorite hymn that left them teary-eyed. And last month there were those moving testimonies during the baptismal service. All resulted in intimate encounters with the Holy Spirit. But all were spaced days or even weeks apart. And, as is usually the case, all were *passive*. All were dependent on the Spirit to initiate the encounter. Most believers rarely think (or even know why they might want) to initiate an intimate encounter with the Holy Spirit.

The *Way of Escape* Battle Plan is all about initiating intimate encounters with the Holy Spirit. And not only on Sunday mornings while seated in a church pew. A daily filling of the Spirit. Or even multiple times a day. As often as the sheltering presence of the Spirit is needed in the war against the flesh. The active pursuit of regular relationship intimacy with the Holy Spirit. This is what sets the *Way of Escape* Battle Plan apart from all other battle plans.

> **KEY REGULARITY: The active pursuit of regular relationship intimacy with the Holy Spirit is the key to unleashing His inner-working power (Ephesians 3:20) and winning the war against the flesh.**

God has indeed made a way for ordinary lay Christians to live victorious lives. In our own strength this would be impossible (Romans 8:3a). But empowered by His Spirit, victorious Christian living is not only possible, it is the expected outcome (Romans 8:4).

This is not about "manning up" to tough out a way of escape. It's all about being more intentional in accessing the Holy Spirit at a more intimate level and allowing Him to lead the escape (Galatians 5:16). It is surprisingly easy to live sexually pure and porn-free when the Holy Spirit is in the lead. Easier than I ever could have asked or thought (Ephesians 3:20). But the Spirit's hands are tied—and the level of difficulty skyrockets—when I limit my asking and thinking to ways of escape that are "me-powered," rather than Spirit-powered.

Walking in the Spirit is the key to repelling attacks of the flesh (Galatians 5:16). Walking in the Spirit is the key to discovering God's promised way of escape from temptation (I Corinthians 10:13). As a born-again believer, I can mortify the deeds of the flesh by choosing to walk in the Spirit (Romans 8:12-13). "But what," the reader asks, "does it mean to be 'walking in the Spirit'? What does 'walking in the Spirit' look like?" Here are but a few examples for the reader's consideration:

> Reading the Bible and prayer head the list. But both are words-only events that, for the addict, are largely ineffective against the limbic (think emotional, visual) attacks of the flesh when it is at peak strength (see *Reprogramming the Brain*, Chapter 2).

- The palpable heart-tugs felt during the pastor's "nailed it" sermon last Sunday
- The lump in the throat during the missionary's slide show the week before
- The Drama Team's moving skit last Easter
- The choir's rendition of a favorite hymn that always brings a tear

In each of these latter four visually oriented, emotion-charged examples, the believer/viewer is, at least for a brief time, walking in the Spirit. During these times, it is impossible to fulfill the lust of the flesh. It is impossible for the choked-up and teary-eyed to fulfill the lust of the flesh, while the Holy Spirit is tugging on their heart (Galatians 5:16).

> **KEY IMPOSSIBILITY:** *It is impossible for the choked-up and teary-eyed to fulfill the lust of the flesh, while the Holy Spirit is tugging on their heart (Galatians 5:16).*

A filling of the Spirit and a lust of the flesh can *never* occur at the same time (Galatians 5:16). Hmmm. If only these "walking in the Spirit" moments could be bottled and instantly recalled whenever the flesh makes an unwanted house call. Good news, dear reader. With today's technology, now they can be.

BUILDING A LIBRARY OF SPIRIT-ANOINTED, FLESH-DIFFUSING APPLICATIONS

Effecting a filling of the Spirit at a moment's notice is the key to repelling surprise attacks of the flesh. But an application that fills one with the Spirit may be completely ineffective for another. "Walking in the Spirit" is not a one-size-fits-all experience. Each born-again believer will have their own unique set of triggers that issue in a filling of the Spirit. Each will therefore have to identify their own unique set of Spirit-anointed, flesh-diffusing applications.

For me, nothing more consistently issues in a filling of the Spirit than selected music videos from the Gaither Homecoming concerts. And I am not alone. Many others have told of similar Spirit-filling experiences. Mr. Gaither gives a fascinating account of the Spirit's moving on that day back in 1991 during taping of the inaugural Homecoming concert.[4] Many of The Homecoming Friends present that day also made mention of the Spirit's unmistakable anointing. What was to be a recording session for a single song turned into a full day of singing, testimonies, prayers, and sweet fellowship. The Spirit was indeed filling as The Homecoming Friends spoke to one another in hymns and spiritual songs, making melody in their hearts to the Lord (Ephesians 5:18b-19). And not only during that initial taping, but countless others have testified of an anointing over the entire Homecoming concert series.

For me, nothing more consistently issues in a filling of the Spirit than selected music videos from the Gaither Homecoming concerts.

All of my Top 16 Spirit-anointed apps are music videos taken from these Gaither Homecoming concerts. My home library currently consists of 1441 video tracks on 53 Gaither Homecoming concert DVDs (see *Appendix E*). Building this library was only the beginning of my research. From this vast collection of music videos, only a very small percentage consistently issue in a filling of the Spirit (for after all, it is certain that the Gaithers did not plan on someone coming in behind them and mining their Homecoming concert DVDs for music videos that tap into the brain's limbic system!). While all tracks on these DVDs aim to edify, not all are intended to evoke a deep emotional response. Of the 1441 Gaither Homecoming video tracks in my possession, only 16 "made the cut" and were included in my library of Spirit-anointed, flesh-diffusing applications.

Interestingly, even of these 16, very few "made the cut" on a first viewing. Even familiar hymns required multiple viewings to take in all the worship taking place in the background, behind the featured onstage artists. It is hard for me to believe now, but *Except for Grace*[5] "missed the cut" on its first few viewings. Multiple viewings over multiple days were required. In time, it did come to consistently issue in a filling of the Spirit and was included in my library of Spirit-anointed, flesh-diffusing apps.

> *KEY INSIGHT: The singing of spiritual songs is one way in which God, via the Spirit, has chosen to intimately connect with His children (Ephesians 5:18b-19). Believer/viewers of these "symphonies of praise" experience the same intimacy. Seeing (limbic visual) the reactions (limbic emotional) of The Homecoming Friends in the background, behind the featured onstage artists. This is the recipe for a believer/viewer to consistently experience the Spirit's filling. Neurologically speaking, these "symphonies of praise" are also supplying the believer/viewer's limbic system with the spiritual content that it needs to reprogram his brain.*

Crucial to "getting" this KEY INSIGHT is recognizing that Ephesians 5:18b-19 is bidirectional. Every commentary that I have read correctly states that the singing of spiritual songs (v. 19) is a natural result when believers are filled with the Spirit (v. 18b). But the reverse is also true. Spirit fillings (v. 18b) are a natural result when believers gather to engage in the singing of spiritual songs (v. 19). All who have been caught up in the Spirit as the choir or congregation sings a favorite hymn confirm this truth. Ephesians 5:18b-19 is indeed bidirectional.

SAFE IN THE SPIRIT

There is safety in the presence of the Holy Spirit (Galatians 5:16). When the flesh attacks (and also long before, for it is this repetitive Spirit-filling in pre-emptive mode that affects the lasting neurological change), run to a place where a filling of the Spirit is experienced and stay there until the danger passes. For me, that place of Spirit-filling is in front of a television monitor, watching select Gaither Homecoming music videos (Ephesians 5:18b-19).

OK for me. But what about you, the reader? Each genuinely born-again reader will have their own unique set of triggers. Each genuinely born-again reader will have their own unique set of places to go to experience a filling of the Spirit. Dear reader, only you know where your places of Spirit-filling are. Your places of Spirit-filling may not include a single Gaither Homecoming music video. Your places of Spirit-filling may not even involve a single application of Ephesians 5:18b-19. Triggers will differ, of course. But the run-to-safety application is the same:

> **When the flesh attacks (and also long before, for it is this repetitive Spirit-filling in pre-emptive mode that affects the lasting neurological change), run to a place where a filling of the Spirit is experienced and stay there until the danger passes.**

7

SPIRIT-ANOINTED, FLESH-DIFFUSING APPLICATIONS

I say then: Walk in the Spirit, and you shall not fulfill the lust of the flesh (Galatians 5:16).

Chapter 6 introduced the *discipline* of "walking in the Spirit." Here in Chapter 7, we look at the *means* of "walking in the Spirit."

If all of the pre-emptive strikes described in Chapters 3-5 are carried out, they will greatly reduce the number of opportunities for the flesh to launch an attack. But the flesh will still occasionally break through. It is for these remaining times that counterattack measures will be needed, measures that are strong in the Spirit, for the shutting down of the flesh.

The literature describes a variety of approaches, all with an eye toward short-circuiting the flesh. Anything that can distract the flesh, for even the briefest of moments, is a possible candidate. Perhaps motivated by David's use of the harp to calm Saul's troubled spirit (I Samuel 16:14-23), some have suggested listening to music. Other suggestions include exercise, diving into a hobby, meditation, reading, and journaling. All that I reviewed recommended incorporating an accountability partner or group at some point in the short-circuiting process.

The *Way of Escape* Battle Plan relies solely on the Holy Spirit's power to deliver believers from lusts of the flesh (Galatians 5:16). In this chapter, construction of a library of fast-acting, Spirit-anointed, flesh-diffusing applications is described. Accessible with the push of a "Play" button, these apps typically require no more than a few minutes to diffuse an attack. I have become so familiar with the attached images that simply hearing the first few notes of the stronger apps will escort me into the Spirit's presence (think Pavlov's dogs), with the escape accomplished in a matter of only seconds, not minutes.

SPIRIT-ANOINTED MUSIC

Throughout the Bible, music is given a significant place in both individual and corporate worship. Early in the biblical chronology, Jubal is recognized as the father of all who play the harp and flute (Genesis 4:21). Scripture also describes how Saul, in the early stages of his fallen state, found comfort for his troubled spirit in music (I Samuel 16:14-23). David made special preparations for music to be incorporated into corporate worship in his plans for the first temple (I Chronicles 25). Even today, across all denominational lines, music continues to play an important role in corporate worship.

In my early days as a Christian, I had looked to music to fend off attacks of the flesh. As I began my search for Spirit-anointed, flesh-diffusing apps for this work, I looked to music once again. If music chased the troubled spirit from Saul, perhaps it could also chase the raging flesh from me.

My favorite CD of Christian songs is Steve Green's *People Need the Lord*.[1] The rising crescendo, present in many of these power anthems, serves as a spiritual call to arms in the battle with the flesh. I would be hard-pressed to find a better set of songs on one CD for fending off attacks of the flesh. But while these power anthems inspire, they do not consistently issue in a Spirit filling, even when the flesh is quiet, and never when the flesh is at full strength.

Why are these great hymns of the faith unable to repel the strong attacks of the flesh? Advances in neuroscience offer a possible explanation. The words of songs, even if deeply spiritual, and even if sung out loud, at best, only lightly engage the brain's limbic system. The flesh fully engages the brain when launching its video attacks. A dominantly words-only counterattack will be largely ineffective against the video attacks of the flesh. For the addict, limbic weaponry (think emotional, visual) is a better choice for repelling the video attacks of the flesh.

The use of video weaponry to win the battle against the flesh makes perfect sense. After all, it was likely years of bludgeoning the brain with pornographic images/videos that first led to the addiction. Reason and neuroscience unite in suggesting that video weaponry is preferred if the battle to overcome porn addiction is to be won. Words (e.g., written text and/or audio CDs), no matter how spiritual, will only very rarely be effective deterrents to "acting out" sexually once the flesh is at full strength.

> **If bludgeoning the brain with pornographic videos is what led to the addiction, then reason and neuroscience unite in suggesting that video weaponry is preferred if the battle to overcome porn addiction is to be won.**

Spirit-anointed music cannot consistently turn back the flesh when it is at peak strength. The impact of Spirit-anointed music videos is examined next.

SPIRIT-ANOINTED MUSIC VIDEOS

Applications lacking an emotional/visual component are largely ineffective at short-circuiting the flesh once it is at full strength. Advances in neuroscience help to explain why. Attacks launched by the flesh incorporate powerful visual components that fully engage the brain. Words-only counterattacks (e.g., a song, or a Scripture passage), no matter how spiritual, at best, only lightly engage the brain's limbic system. If the flesh is to be consistently short-circuited when at full strength, my spiritual weaponry must include a strong emotional/visual component.

But which medium will be the most effective? Will it be a series of moving sermons set against a carefully orchestrated series of images? Or perhaps selected scenes from a series of particularly touching Christian movies? Or maybe a collection of music videos? And if the latter, is the genre contemporary Christian, inspirational, or Southern Gospel? One size will not fit all. Everyone is wired differently. What short-circuits the flesh for one may be completely ineffective for another. For me, and the way in which I am wired, no one more effectively blends the emotional/visual and the spiritual than the Gaither Music Group.

> *No one more effectively blends the emotional/visual and the spiritual than the Gaither Music Group.*

Indeed, each of the Top 16 entries in my library of Spirit-anointed, flesh-diffusing apps are taken from the Gaither Homecoming concert series. I have found that nothing more effectively sets the spiritual stage than a gathering of Christians engaged in unrehearsed, sincere acts of worship (*). A filling of the Spirit is assured if, as the camera pans the stage/audience, it happens to catch a teary-eyed worshipper already caught up in the Spirit. This is the "worship formula" that most consistently issues in a filling of the Spirit in me. And no one bottles this "worship formula" better than the Gaither Music Group.

(*) Though it often displays as nothing more than a raised hand, when I use the expression "act(s) of worship," I am referring to a more animated moving of the Spirit that results in worshippers: (i) fighting back or shedding tears, (ii) fist-pumping, or (iii) uttering a Spirit-inspired cry of praise.

MY LIBRARY OF 23 SPIRIT-ANOINTED, FLESH-DIFFUSING APPLICATIONS

From my library of 53 Homecoming concert DVDs (see Appendix E), I have identified 16 music videos that consistently escort me into the presence of the Holy Spirit. These music videos are ranked according to their Spirit-filling strength, which, for me, is a mix of the following ingredients:

- Creating an atmosphere of genuine corporate worship (all 16 apps)
- Worshippers moved by the Spirit to tears (apps 1-12)
- Songs aptly described as power anthems (apps 13-16)

This three-point ranking criterion (along with the descriptions to follow) also doubles as a blueprint for how I went about creating my library of Spirit-anointed, flesh-diffusing apps. The interested reader may wish to use this blueprint, or some variation thereof, as a starting point for creation of their own library.

Corporate Worship Atmosphere: There is a common thread running through this library of 16 apps—The Homecoming Friends engaged in unrehearsed, highly emotional, highly visual acts of worship, in the background, behind the featured onstage artists. It is no coincidence that each of these 16 apps feature The Homecoming Friends in precisely this role. These highly emotional and highly visual acts are an essential ingredient in the "worship formula" that most readily issues in a filling of the Spirit in me.

Moved by the Spirit to Tears: Music videos where the camera catches either a Homecoming Friend or audience member teary-eyed shoot to the top of my rankings. Without fail, when the Holy Spirit moves a fellow believer to tears, He will use that emotional/visual act of worship to also draw me into His presence (see KEY INSIGHT, Chapter 6). Neurologically speaking, seeing (limbic visual) a fellow believer moved to tears (limbic emotional) accesses my limbic system with the spiritual content that it needs to reprogram my brain (again, see KEY INSIGHT, Chapter 6). Each of my Top 12 apps include some form of this Spirit filling.

Neurologically speaking, seeing (limbic visual) a fellow believer moved to tears (limbic emotional)

*accesses my limbic system with the spiritual content
that it needs to reprogram my brain.*

Power Anthems: Then there are those songs that unleash pure
Spirit power (apps 13-16). I may not get teary-eyed. But these songs
always deliver a powerful, emotion-packed heart-tug that leaves me
feeling like I could run through a brick wall for Christ.

Each of these 16 Spirit-anointed apps were used quite extensively in
pre-emptive mode to renew my mind—and to keep it renewed. Even
now, to calm my mind from the events of the day, I will immerse myself
in the Spirit by watching these apps for 30-60 minutes most evenings (see
Appendix E for four sample playlists).

These first 16 apps include video footage dating as far back as 1995.
To these, I have added seven (7) more Spirit-anointed apps that feature
a mix of Christian-based choirs/groups (apps 17-19), dramatic
presentations (apps 20-21), and movie scenes (apps 22-23). Apps with
"more modern" video footage. Apps that, in keeping with God's recipe
for experiencing a filling of the Spirit, are each overlaid with an
appropriate spiritual song (Ephesians 5:18b-19; see also KEY INSIGHT,
Chapter 6).

Together then, these are the 23 Spirit-anointed, flesh-diffusing apps
that I use to regularly experience relationship intimacy with the Holy
Spirit (see list, page opposite). Good-bye passivity. Hello run-to-safety
immersions in the Spirit. Immersions that allow me to daily—and even
moment-by-moment (if necessary)—escape lusts of the flesh (Galatians
5:16). An escape that, most notably, has never required enlisting the aid
of an accountability partner or group.

Dear reader, God has promised that there is a way of escape from
every temptation (I Corinthians 10:13). Spirit-anointed music videos are
an essential ingredient in my Escape Plan. Might they also be that one
key missing ingredient in your quest for sexual purity?

My Top 23 Spirit-Anointed Apps

Gaither Homecoming Concert Music Videos

1. A Few Good Men
2. Then Came the Morning
3. Worthy the Lamb
4. The Old Rugged Cross Made the Difference
5. Four Days Late
6. Except for Grace
7. He Saw Me
8. Yes, I Know
9. The Night Before Easter
10. Master of the Wind
11. Another Soldier's Coming Home
12. I Am Not Ashamed
13. Through the Fire
14. He's Alive
15. Let Freedom Ring
16. I've Just Seen Jesus

Choirs/Groups, Dramatic Presentations, and Movie Scenes Overlaid with Spiritual Song

17. Is He Worthy?
18. What a Beautiful Name
19. Thank You Jesus for the Blood
20. Everything
21. How He Loves
22. Mary, Did You Know?
23. Revelation Song

The interested reader can view all 23 of my apps on *YouTube*. The title of my publicly shared playlist is "A Way of Escape: Top 23 Spirit-Anointed Apps."

#1 - A Few Good Men
(Suzanne Jennings, Barry Jennings
/ Townsend and Warbucks Music)

For the eyes of the Lord run to and fro throughout the whole earth, to show Himself strong in the behalf of them whose heart is perfect toward Him … (II Chronicles 16:9 - KJV)

Produced in New York City's Carnegie Hall shortly after the 2001 terrorist attacks on the twin towers, the *Let Freedom Ring* Homecoming concert rendition[2] deftly blends patriotism with a spiritual call to arms. This app begins with the latter, as the believer/viewer is reminded of our dying world, so desperately in need of a few good men of God. A challenge has been issued. There are open positions on God's Special Operations Team. He is searching for those few whose hearts are pure, for it is through these that He most delights in demonstrating His strength and power (II Chronicles 16:9). The believer/viewer's heart warms as the Holy Spirit beckons, "Yes, you too can be one of these select individuals, mightily used by God." The flesh, raging just moments before, is already weakening.

Yes, God is looking for a few good men. A tip of the hat to the Gaither Music Group for the atmosphere that they have created in this music video. The believer/viewer is firmly convinced that the six men leading this worship song are six such good men, evidenced by the approving facial expressions as the camera pans the audience at the 1:25 mark. The Holy Spirit uses these approving looks to further warm the believer/viewer's heart to the uplifting message of the song, and the godly men delivering it.

As the song launches into a third chorus, five members of the New York Firefighters for Christ enter from stage left—men who just months before had been involved in rescue efforts where the twin towers once stood. This Spirit-fired blend of worship and patriotism brings the Homecoming Friends and a roaring audience to their collective feet. The flesh, so strong just a few minutes before, is in full retreat. As the camera pans the stage, it catches a couple of The Homecoming Friends shedding tears. Several of our firefighting heroes, overwhelmed by the outpouring of love, are also fighting to hold back the tears. Later, as our heroes exit stage left, the camera catches several members of the audience also wiping away tears. What a sight. Hundreds of men and women engaged in unrehearsed, genuine acts of worship. The Holy Spirit seizes upon such acts by once more tugging on the believer/viewer's heart (see KEY INSIGHT, Chapter 6). And what has become of the flesh? It has been sent packing by a rousing, visually powerful, Spirit-anointed, flesh-obliterating rendition of *A Few Good Men.*

> **The flesh has been sent packing by a rousing, visually powerful, Spirit-anointed, flesh-obliterating rendition of A Few Good Men.**

By song's end, I have joined the choked-up and teary-eyed. I am walking in the Spirit, and so long as I continue walking with Him (press "Repeat Chapter" as often as needed), I cannot possibly fulfill the lust of the flesh (Galatians 5:16). Thank you, Holy Spirit!

#2 - Then Came the Morning
(William J. & Gloria Gaither, Chris Christian
/ Gaither Music Company, Home Sweet Home Music)

This powerful, heart-tugging hymn has appeared on three (3) different Homecoming concert DVDs (*Whispering Hope*, *Canadian*, and *The Old Rugged Cross*). For me, the renditions that most readily issue in a filling of the Spirit are those that catch one or more of The Homecoming Friends caught up in the Spirit, in the background, behind the featured onstage artist(s). Invariably, the Spirit will use these unrehearsed, emotion-charged acts of worship to also draw me into His presence (see KEY INSIGHT, Chapter 6). I chose to add the *Whispering Hope* rendition[3] to my library of Spirit-anointed apps, because, of the three renditions noted above, it best captures this Spirit-anointed corporate worship atmosphere.

The lead artist delivers with his usual power as he describes in song the emotional roller coaster the disciples must have experienced on that first Easter Weekend. But for me, the "star" of this music video enters over his right shoulder, as the camera captures one of The Homecoming Friends in unscripted acts of worship around the 0:50, 1:25, and 2:30 marks. Caught up in the Spirit, she is fighting back the tears as the lyrics of the song remind her once more of Christ's victory over death on Resurrection Sunday Morning. The Holy Spirit will seize upon her genuine heartfelt acts of worship to also grab hold of my heart. In a matter of minutes, the Holy Spirit (the real "star" of this music video) has been summoned, and the flesh repelled. Once the Spirit has gained the upper hand, repeated plays build a spiritual barrier that the flesh has no chance of breaking through (Galatians 5:16). Thank you, Holy Spirit!

Once the Spirit has gained the upper hand, repeated plays build a spiritual barrier that the flesh has no chance of breaking through (Galatians 5:16).

#3 - Worthy the Lamb
(William J. & Gloria Gaither / Gaither Music Company)

Then I looked, and I heard the voice of many angels around the throne ... Saying ... "Worthy is the Lamb who was slain to receive power and riches and wisdom, and strength and honor and glory and blessing!" (Revelation 5:11a, 12)

This song is featured on two (2) Homecoming concert DVDs (*Freedom Band* and *South African*). I chose to add the *South African* Homecoming rendition[4] to my library of Spirit-anointed apps for its beautiful illustration of the "worship formula" (see *Spirit-Anointed Music Videos*, earlier here in Chapter 7) that the Spirit so often uses to escort me into His presence.

Always a moving hymn, the *South African* Homecoming rendition gets an added boost from the lead artists. Touched by the words of the story he is voicing in song, one of the onstage artists is overtaken by the Spirit. Teary-eyed and voice failing, he manages to collect himself, and make it to the chorus, where he is joined by his three onstage co-artists. By song's end, another of the onstage artists is similarly overtaken. The Holy Spirit has used the shed tears of one believer to draw another into His presence. This is the "worship formula" that most readily issues in a filling of the Spirit in me, and it is playing out, right before my eyes, in this music video.

> *This is the "worship formula" that most readily issues in a filling of the Spirit in me, and it is playing out, right before my eyes, in this music video.*

The Holy Spirit will then use these two unrehearsed acts of worship to draw the viewer into His presence. For the genuinely born-again believer who may still be struggling to fully overcome an addiction, there is no better place to be. So long as he remains sheltered in the Spirit (press "Repeat Chapter" as often as needed), he cannot possibly fulfill the lust of the flesh (Galatians 5:16).

#4 - The Old Rugged Cross Made the Difference
(William J. & Gloria Gaither / Gaither Music Company)

For the message of the cross is foolishness to those who are perishing, but to us who are being saved it is the power of God (I Corinthians 1:18).

Save for a compilation video, this moving tribute to the impact of the Cross appears on only the *London* Homecoming concert DVD.[5] For context and to fully appreciate the fellow artist's reactions to the song, please watch *Rex Nelon Tribute*[6] one track before on this same DVD.

The song lyrics were especially poignant that evening in London, as, just prior to its singing, Mr. Gaither announced that The Homecoming Friends had lost one of their own the night before. With thoughts of their dear friend now listening and watching from above, the Spirit was particularly free to move and touch hearts that evening.

> *With thoughts of their dear friend now listening and watching from above, the Spirit was particularly free to move and touch hearts that evening.*

And did He ever. As the camera pans the stage, most shots catch at least one of The Homecoming Friends shedding a tear. As with so many of these apps, the Holy Spirit will then use these unrehearsed, heartfelt acts of worship to grab hold of other hearts—other of The Homecoming Friends and mine. And once in the Spirit's protective care, I cannot possibly fulfill the lust of the flesh (Galatians 5:16). Thank you, Holy Spirit!

#5 - Four Days Late
(C. Aaron Wilburn, Roberta Wilburn / Winkin' Music,
Darby Corner Music, House of Aaron Music)

**Now when He had said these things, He cried with a loud voice, "Lazarus, come forth!" And he who had died came out bound hand and foot with graveclothes, and his face was wrapped with a cloth. Jesus said to them, "Loose him, and let him go."
(John 11:43-44)**

A beautiful—but lesser-known—song, this moving account of the raising of Lazarus (John 11:1-45) is included on only the *I'll Fly Away* Homecoming concert DVD.[7]

Her voice quivering on several occasions, the featured onstage artist is clearly moved by the Spirit as she recounts this uplifting story of Jesus' power over death. The Spirit seizes upon her heartfelt act of worship to draw others—myself and other of The Homecoming Friends—into His presence (see KEY INSIGHT, Chapter 6). The flesh is in retreat. With the Spirit tugging on hearts, there is no longer a place for the flesh to gain a foothold (Galatians 5:16).

The lead artist then closes with a powerful dose of pure Spirit power. We are first softly reminded that Jesus has not changed. Though it might seem as though He is absent in the middle of my struggle, via the Spirit, He is just as near now as He was in Lazarus' day. Crescendo rising, she then triumphantly proclaims that Jesus is still rolling back stones and still calling besieged believers by name. Wow! In true Lazarus-like fashion, these wonderfully uplifting lyrics raise both The Homecoming Friends and the audience to their collective feet. If by faith believed, how sweet this message must also sound to the genuinely born-again believer who may still be struggling to fully overcome an addiction.

Though it might seem as though He is absent in the middle of my struggle, via the Spirit, Jesus is just as near now as he was in Lazarus' day.

#6 – Except for Grace
(Jeff Silvey / Word Music, Big Ole Hit Music, Curb Songs)

For by grace you have been saved through faith, and that not of yourselves; it is the gift of God, Not of works, lest anyone should boast (Ephesians 2:8-9).

Another of those beautiful—but lesser-known—songs, this moving account of God's saving grace is included on only the *Good News* Homecoming concert DVD.[8]

We are reminded of sin's devastating consequences in each of the first two verses. But all to make God's grace appear the more gracious. And does this formula ever work. The Homecoming Friends fall silent with each mention of sin's devastation. Most seem to be quietly reflecting on their own failings; some are saddened to the point of tears. But all gives way to joy and cries of praise as each chorus reminds of God's forgiving love and saving grace! The closing verse reminds that our best attempts to amend can never pay the price for our sins. We are all hopelessly lost, were it not for grace. All boasting aside, it is by God's grace—and *only* by God's grace—that we can have our sins blotted out and be saved (Ephesians 2:8-9).

This music video cannot help but tug on the hearts of all who have acknowledged their sin and experienced God's forgiving love and saving grace. And this is precisely what the recovering addict needs in a time of temptation. With the Spirit tugging on his heart, the flesh must flee (Galatians 5:16). And so long as he remains immersed in the Spirit (press "Repeat Chapter" as often as needed), he cannot possibly fulfill the lust of the flesh (again, Galatians 5:16).

> *... this is precisely what the recovering addict needs in a time of temptation... so long as he remains immersed in the Spirit... he cannot possibly fulfill the lust of the flesh (Galatians 5:16).*

#7 - He Saw Me
(Joan Ewing / Landy Ewing Publishing)

Your eyes saw my substance, being yet unformed. And in Your book they all were written, the days fashioned for me, when as yet there were none of them (Psalm 139:16).

Yet another one of those lesser-known songs featured at a Homecoming concert, this mesmerizing take on God's love appears on only the *Rivers of Joy* DVD.[9]

A master of the dramatic pause and softly measured words, the lead artist engages the viewer in a way unlike any of the other apps reviewed in this work. As the song title suggests, the lyrics also let *every* viewer know that this message of God's love, while it applies to whosoever hears and believes (John 3:16), is also deeply personal. That sound heard when the lead artist, with voice failing, softly sings, "... He saw me." Why, that's the sound of hearts melting!

> *That sound heard when the lead artist, with voice failing, softly sings, "... He saw me." Why, that's the sound of hearts melting!*

Dear reader, insert *Rivers of Joy* into your DVD player (or pull up its playlist on *YouTube*). Watch *He Saw Me*, and let the lyrics really sink in. Take in the looks of the fully engaged Homecoming Friends. Revel in the Spirit as He begins to well up within. He is in the process of engineering your escape right now—in real time! Watch a second time, picking up on still more worship taking place in the background, behind the featured artist. Rewind for a third watch. By now your brain knows what's coming. The heart-tugs don't even wait for the lyrics or images; they have already begun as the opening notes of the song are played (think Pavlov's dogs). The spiritual reaction is complete. You are walking in the Spirit, and so long as you stay immersed in the Spirit (press "Repeat Chapter" as often as needed), you cannot possibly fulfill lusts of the flesh (Galatians 5:16).

#8 – Yes, I Know
(Anna W. Waterman / Gaither Vocal Band arrangers, Gaither Music Company)

This heart-tugging, head-bobbing, toe-tapping song is featured on five (5) different Homecoming concert DVDs (*Texas Style, Feelin' at Home, Gospel Bluegrass Volume I, Campfire,* and *Tent Revival*). The mini-revival that breaks out mid-song in the *Feelin' at Home* rendition[10] made it the easy choice for inclusion in my library of Spirit-anointed, flesh-diffusing apps.

> *The mini-revival that breaks out mid-song in the* Feelin' at Home *rendition[10] made it the easy choice for inclusion in my library of Spirit-anointed apps.*

The Gaithers usually produced 2-3 DVDs from the material created at each of their Homecoming concerts. The *Feelin' at Home* and *Joy in the Camp* DVDs—which feature my #8, #9, and #10-ranked apps—were part of the same Spirit-anointed gathering. It is not difficult to understand how revival could have broken out at some point during these tapings. How sweet the presence of the Spirit must have been throughout. Surely He was filling as The Homecoming Friends spoke to one another in spiritual songs, while singing and making melody in their hearts to the Lord (Ephesians 5:18b-19).

The Spirit-anointed corporate worship atmosphere captured during this song is unrivaled on the 53 Homecoming concert DVDs in my possession. There were more camera shots of Homecoming Friends wiping away tears than I could count. Nowhere in my library of 23 apps are Spirit movings better captured on camera than in these tears and in the multiple cannot-stay-seated mid-song cries of The Homecoming Friends. Finally, the third verse lyrics describing Jesus' role (in conjunction with the Holy Spirit) in holding the flesh at bay during temptation serves up desperately needed biblical truth for the believer still struggling to fully overcome an addiction. Outstanding!

#9 - The Night Before Easter
(Donnie Sumner, Duane Friend / Gospel Quartet Music)

**And behold, there was a great earthquake;
for an angel of the Lord descended from heaven, and came and
rolled back the stone from the door ... (Matthew 28:2)**

This song was featured at both the *London* and *Joy in the Camp*[11] Homecomings. I chose to go with the latter, as it also included the lead artist's teary-eyed testimony[12] two tracks before on this same DVD.

Having shared his testimony just minutes before, the lead artist, still caught up in the Spirit, struggles to hold it together before collecting himself to deliver a powerful and triumphant close. I also counted no less than 14 near-camera shots of Homecoming Friends either fighting back or wiping away tears. Outstanding! The Spirit will use these unrehearsed, emotion-charged acts of worship to draw me into His presence (see KEY INSIGHT, Chapter 6). Watched in conjunction with this artist's testimony two tracks before, even after countless viewings, this one-two punch still never fails to effect a filling of the Spirit in me.

Neurologically speaking, each viewing bombards my limbic system with the highly emotional, highly visual spiritual content that it needs to reprogram my brain (see *Reprogramming the Brain*, Chapter 2). And with each repeated viewing, these healthier Spirit-anointed neural pathways deepen, while the unhealthy, now-idle (according to the promise of Galatians 5:16) fleshly neural pathways are pruned back. With each viewing of *Testimony / The Night Before Easter*, my mind is being renewed by the transforming ministry of the Holy Spirit (Romans 12:2).

With each viewing of **Testimony / The Night Before Easter**, *my mind is being renewed by the transforming ministry of the Holy Spirit (Romans 12:2).*

#10 - Master of the Wind
(Joel Hemphill / Family and Friends Music,
Hemphill Music Company)

Then He arose and rebuked the wind, and said to the sea, "Peace, be still!" And the wind ceased and there was a great calm. But He said to them, "Why are you so fearful? How is it that you have no faith?" And they feared exceedingly, and said to one another, "Who can this be, that even the wind and the sea obey Him!" (Mark 4:39-41)

Still another of those beautiful—but lesser-known—songs, *Master of the Wind* is included on only the *Joy in the Camp* Homecoming DVD.[13] For context and to fully appreciate the fellow artist's reactions to this song, please watch *Testimony*[12] one track before on this same DVD.

One of the more tenderhearted of The Homecoming Friends, the lead artist is the perfect choice to deliver the highly emotional, highly visual spiritual content that the viewer's limbic system needs to renew his mind and reprogram his brain (see *Reprogramming the Brain*, Chapter 2). And does she ever deliver. Right out of the gate she is fighting back the tears as the opening lyrics remind her of the Friend she has in Jesus when the storms of life descend. The camera does a masterful job of setting the spiritual stage for the balance of this music video by first capturing the immediate reactions of her proud parents and then that of the author of *Testimony*. My limbic system was being fed throughout, as I counted at least seven (7) near-camera shots of Homecoming Friends either fighting back or wiping away tears. Once again, I say, "Outstanding!"

> *One of the more tenderhearted of The Homecoming Friends, the lead artist is the perfect choice to deliver the highly emotional, highly visual spiritual content that the viewer's limbic system needs to renew his mind and reprogram his brain.*

#11 - Another Soldier's Coming Home
(Janet Paschal / Maplesong Music, BMM Music)

I have fought the good fight, I have finished the race, I have kept the faith. Finally, there is laid up for me the crown of righteousness, which the Lord, the righteous Judge, will give to me on that Day, and not to me only but also to all who have loved His appearing (II Timothy 4:7-8).

Initially featured on *Marching to Zion*[14], this wonderfully moving song also appears on *The Best of Janet Paschal from the Homecoming Series.*[15]

Like so many of the pre-2000 Homecoming concerts, this is one of those tapings where the "audience" was composed entirely of fellow artists. With most every member of the audience acquainted with (or themselves) a frontline soldier, this song really resonated with its listeners. Nearly all are visibly moved by the Spirit in this captivating music video—I counted no less than 15 near-camera shots of audience members either fighting back or wiping away tears. Sowing in tears, The Homecoming Friends shall one day doubtless reap in joy, bringing their Spirit-anointed, tear-bought sheaves with them (Psalm 126:5-6). As an eternally grateful benefactor of their tears, I say, "Thank you, dear tenderhearted Homecoming Friends!"

This is also another one of those apps for which I have become so familiar with the accompanying emotionally charged images that oftentimes just hearing the first few notes of this song will escort me into the Spirit's presence (think Pavlov's dogs), with the escape accomplished in a matter of only seconds, not minutes.

I have become so familiar with the accompanying emotionally charged images that oftentimes just hearing the first few notes of this song will escort me into the Spirit's presence (think Pavlov's dogs), with the escape accomplished in a matter of only seconds, not minutes.

#12 - I Am Not Ashamed
(Dawn Thomas / McSpadden Music)

For I am not ashamed of the gospel of Christ, for it is the power of God to salvation for everyone who believes, for the Jew first and also for the Greek (Romans 1:16).

At the height of its popularity in the early 1990s, this song introduced the lead singer as a solo artist to audiences nationwide. First featured on the *All Day Singin' and Dinner on the Ground* Homecoming DVD[16], it also appears on *The Best of Janet Paschal from the Homecoming Series.*[17]

This is one of those songs that speaks to most every believer, but particularly to those that have made unashamedly proclaiming the Gospel their life's work. Another of those pre-2000 Homecoming concerts, *All Day Singin' and Dinner on the Ground* (1995) was taped in-studio, with the "audience" composed entirely of fellow artists. With each member of the audience themselves active in proclaiming the Gospel, this song had tremendous heart appeal, evidenced by the many approving nods and mesmerized looks the camera captures as it pans the stage. Young and old, male and female, new artists and seasoned Southern Gospel greats—nearly all are visibly moved by the Spirit in the music video rendition of this popular 1990s song.

> *Young and old, male and female, new artists and seasoned Southern Gospel greats—nearly all are visibly moved by the Spirit in the music video rendition of this popular 1990s song.*

#13 – Through the Fire
(Gerald D. Crabb / Crabb's Song Music)

... When you walk through the fire, you shall not be burned, nor shall the flame scorch you (Isaiah 43:2b).

Included on the *New Orleans* Homecoming concert DVD[18], the featured family of onstage artists takes the viewer on a raucous, inspiring ride, paying tribute to both our Lord Jesus Christ and the Holy Spirit for the many through-the-fire victories won over our adversary, the wicked one.

The lead artist doesn't just sing praises; he grinds them out. This is not the tale of a war-weary soldier hoisting a white flag but of a battle-tested warrior putting his foot to the throat of the enemy. And does it ever work. More than just nice words to a song, the viewer is convinced that the lead artist is not giving a second-hand account but that he has personally experienced these through-the-fire victories. Caught up in the Spirit, the viewer dares to believe, "It has worked for him. Perhaps God has provided a way of escape for me after all."

Caught up in the Spirit, the viewer dares to believe, "It has worked for him. Perhaps God has provided a way of escape for me after all."

By song's end, I am looking for a brick wall to run through for Christ. And I am not alone. The Homecoming Friends have risen to their collective feet, and, reminiscent of a secular concert, the audience does not stop applauding until the onstage artists return for an encore. What a wildly fun ride for all.

I never tire of hearing this song's uplifting message or of the family of onstage artists that so passionately delivers it. And how encouraging to know that all the repeated viewings in pre-emptive mode are also creating healthier (and deepening existing) neural pathways that will dramatically reduce the number of future enemy attacks (see *Reprogramming the Brain*, Chapter 2). Outstanding!

#14 - He's Alive
(Don Francisco / New Spring Publishing)

This power anthem is featured on two (2) Homecoming concert DVDs (*Journey to the Sky*, and *Tent Revival*). The *Tent Revival* Homecoming concert rendition[19] is electric, which made it an easy choice for inclusion in my library of Spirit-anointed, flesh-diffusing applications.

This moving story of the first Easter Weekend, told from Peter's perspective, was first released in 1977. Thinking that the lyrics might be sufficiently moving to short-circuit the flesh, I had screened the audio version of *He's Alive*[20] back when I first began considering candidates for inclusion in my library of Spirit-anointed apps. However, much like the Steve Green CD of hymns[1], *He's Alive*, in audio format, did not consistently issue in a Spirit filling, even when the flesh was quiet, and never when the flesh was at full strength.

This tale then took a most interesting turn. As I was building my library of Gaither Homecoming DVDs, I discovered that the *Tent Revival* Homecoming concert featured a music video version of *He's Alive*. With the lead onstage artist delivering with his usual power, and backed by 140-plus fully engaged Homecoming Friends, the Holy Spirit was now welling up within with each viewing. How interesting. Initially rejected as a candidate for my library of Spirit-anointed apps, *He's Alive* had just been resurrected. A song that had proven to be ineffective in words-only (audio CD) format, was now, in video form, consistently issuing in a filling of the Spirit. Though far from a thorough scientific study of the subject, here was at least some initial data suggesting that a *video* antidote is preferred to overcome a *video* addiction.

Here was some initial data suggesting that a* video *antidote is preferred to overcome a* video *addiction.

There is more to this intriguing story. The current app, in audio format, rarely issues in a Spirit filling when played in pre-emptive mode, even while the flesh is quiet. But what about some of the other more powerful apps?

Once my library was finalized, I purchased audio CDs of the same Gaither Homecoming concerts that feature my Top 16 Spirit-anointed music video apps. Interestingly, none had the same emotion-packed, Spirit-filling impact as their music video counterparts on the Homecoming concert DVDs (the reader can verify this reduction in emotional and Spirit-filling impact by simply "watching" the music videos a second time with eyes closed). This simple little experiment demonstrated that the visually oriented Spirit-anointed apps enhance access to the limbic system, the brain's emotional seat (enhance, that is, relative to an audio version of the same app). And because access to the limbic system is enhanced, so too is the volume of spiritual content being piped in to reprogram the brain.

One would think that my most powerful apps—several of which are consistently able to invoke a Pavlovian-dog-type filling of the Holy Spirit with just their first few notes—would issue in a similar filling when played in audio form. But they do not. My brain knows that the emotionally charged images accompanying the music videos are absent on the audio CDs. It cannot be fooled into a Pavlovian-dog-type reaction when the audio CD version begins playing. More evidence perhaps suggesting that a *video* antidote is preferred to overcome a *video* addiction. But I leave this for other author/researchers and another time.

#15 – Let Freedom Ring
(Gloria Gaither, William J. Gaither / Gaither Music Company)

Then Jesus said to those Jews who believed Him, "If you abide in My word, you are My disciples indeed. And you shall know the truth, and the truth shall make you free... if the Son makes you free, you shall be free indeed." (John 8:31-32, 36)

This music video has been featured on three (3) Homecoming concert DVDs (*Oh My Glory*, *Let Freedom Ring*, and *Build a Bridge*). I am partial to the *Let Freedom Ring* rendition[21], for it was while watching it over the 2017 July Fourth Weekend (along with my #1-ranked Spirit-anointed app, *A Few Good Men*, on this same DVD), and experiencing its Spirit-filling effect, that I was first inspired to write this book. A subsequent study of Scripture passages on the Holy Spirit led to my "Galatians 5:16 Revelation" several months later. Having "cut my *Way of Escape* teeth" on this rendition made it the easy choice for inclusion in my library of Spirit-anointed, flesh-diffusing apps.

We all yearn for freedom. God has built a longing for freedom into all of creation. But as passionate as we are about our personal freedoms, God had something far greater in mind—that all might experience the blood-bought everlasting freedom purchased by Christ at Calvary.

The passion and power that the onstage artists bring to this Spirit-fired message brings The Homecoming Friends to their collective feet. As the Spirit wells up within, He is bringing both them and me to a place where we cannot possibly fulfill the lust of the flesh (Galatians 5:16). The very freedom described in song is being carried out by the Holy Spirit—*in real time*! Outstanding!

> *The very freedom described in song is being carried out by the Holy Spirit—***in real time!**

#16 - I've Just Seen Jesus
(Gloria Gaither, William J. Gaither, Danny Daniels
/ Gaither Music Company, Ariose Music)

Jesus said to her, "Woman, why are you weeping? Whom are you seeking?" She, supposing Him to be the gardener, said to Him, "Sir, if You have carried Him away, tell me where You have laid Him, and I will take Him away." Jesus said to her, "Mary!" She turned and said to Him, "Rabboni!" (which is to say, Teacher) ... Mary Magdalene came and told the disciples that she had seen the Lord ... (John 20:15-16, 18a)

This musical account of Mary Magdalene's encounter with Christ at the tomb is featured on two (2) Homecoming concert DVDs (*Kennedy Center* and *Majesty*). The *Kennedy Center* Homecoming concert rendition[22] is electric, making it the easy choice for inclusion in my library of Spirit-anointed, flesh-diffusing apps. The audience found it similarly electric that evening at the Kennedy Center, evidenced by the minute-plus, post-song standing ovation (longer live; it cut out at 70 seconds on the DVD).

This is one of those songs that speaks to most every believer. With two of the 1980s most popular Christian recording artists in the lead, the inspiring lyrics moved many of the Homecoming Friends to clap and cheer. Some shed tears. A few exploded out of their seats with fists pumping. By song's end, most were looking for a brick wall to run through for Christ.

> *By song's end, most were looking for a brick wall to run through for Christ.*

Perhaps *I've Just Seen Jesus* should be ranked higher, for this is yet another of those apps where I have become so familiar with the attached images and emotion-charged message to come that simply hearing the first few notes/words will escort me into the Spirit's presence (think Pavlov's dogs). Thank you, Holy Spirit.

#17 – Is He Worthy?
(Andrew Peterson, Ben Shive / Sparrow Records)

So I wept much, because no one was found worthy to open and read the scroll ... But one of the elders said to me, "Do not weep. Behold, the Lion of the tribe of Judah, the Root of David, has prevailed to open the scroll and to loose its seven seals." (Revelation 5:4-5)

It was noted in the previous chapter that very few of these apps "made the cut" on a first viewing. Multiple viewings are usually required to take in all of the Spirit's movings captured by the camera. Not so with the current app. It "made the cut" and was added to my library of Spirit-anointed apps on its very first viewing.

Is He Worthy?[23] is my #1 app of the "more modern" video footage type. Perhaps it should be #1 overall. Without fail, the Holy Spirit has my heart in a headlock with each and every viewing. Without fail. Every single time.

> *Without fail, the Holy Spirit has my heart in a headlock with each and every viewing. Without fail. Every single time.*

There is something wonderfully uplifting about seeing a group of young persons from differing backgrounds and ethnicities united in a song of praise and adoration to our Savior, the Lord Jesus Christ. The knowing nods. The smiling eyes. The faces aglow. None playing to the camera. And yet the camera captures each engaged in sincere, heartfelt worship of our most Worthy Savior. Outstanding!

Yes, this is yet another of those apps where simply hearing the first few notes of the song is sufficient to escort me into the Spirit's presence (think Pavlov's dogs). And so long as I remain immersed in Him (return the clip to 0:00, and replay as often as needed), I cannot possibly fulfill the lust of the flesh (Galatians 5:16). Thank you, Holy Spirit!

JESUS

#18 – What a Beautiful Name
(Ben Fielding, Brooke Ligertwood / Hillsong Music Publishing)

Let this mind be in you which was also in Christ Jesus, Who, being in the form of God, did not consider it robbery to be equal with God, But made Himself of no reputation, taking the form of a bondservant, and coming in the likeness of men. And being found in appearance as a man, He humbled Himself and became obedient to the point of death, even the death of the cross. Therefore God also has highly exalted Him and given Him the name which is above every name (Philippians 2:5-9)

My library of Spirit-anointed apps would be incomplete without an entry from Hillsong Worship, the Australian praise and worship group. *Shout to the Lord* (1993) is familiar to most adult readers above the age of 40. Founded in 1983, 15 of their songs have appeared on the *Billboard* magazine charts in the United States, with *What a Beautiful Name*[24] representing their greatest success to date (over 425 million *YouTube* views as of January 2022).

Indeed, there is something about that name! Paul rejoiced, even when the name of Jesus was preached insincerely, whether from a spirit of envy and strife or selfish ambition. He rejoiced whenever Jesus was preached, whether in pretense or in truth (Philippians 1:15-18). How he would rejoice at the 20-plus mentions of the names of Jesus included in this wonderfully uplifting praise song. What a beautiful name. And what a beautiful spiritual song (Ephesians 5:19).

What then? Only that in every way, whether in pretense or in truth, Christ is preached; and in this I rejoice, yes, and will rejoice (Philippians 1:18).

#19 – Thank You Jesus for the Blood
(Charity Gayle, Ryan Kennedy, Steven Musso, David Gentiles, Bryan McCleery / Watershed Music)

Giving thanks to the Father who has qualified us to be partakers of the inheritance of the saints in the light. He has delivered us from the power of darkness and conveyed us into the kingdom of the Son of His love, In whom we have redemption through His blood, the forgiveness of sins... For it pleased the Father that in Him all the fullness should dwell, And by Him to reconcile all things to Himself, by Him, whether things on earth or things in heaven, having made peace through the blood of His cross (Colossians 1:12-14, 19-20).

Another favorite contemporary worship song, *Thank You Jesus for the Blood*[25] sings the praises of Jesus' sacrifice for my sin. Thank you Jesus for the blood. The blood shed at Calvary for the forgiveness of my sins. For without the shedding of Your blood there is no remission of my sins (Hebrews 9:22).

A melancholy beginning, as the lead artist reflects on her wretched life before encountering Christ. Crescendo rises at the realization that He has paid her sin debt, conquered the grave, and provided her with the promise of eternal life. Transitioning at last to a song of praise and thanksgiving for the wonder-working power of the blood that transforms lost sinners into sons and daughters of the Most High. What power is on display when Christ, via the Spirit, dwells in the midst of two or three (or more) gathered together in His name (Matthew 18:20).

What power is on display when Christ, via the Spirit, dwells in the midst of two or three (or more) gathered together in His name (Matthew 18:20).

#20 – Everything
(Jason Wade / Dreamworks)

"The thief does not come except to steal, and to kill, and to destroy. I have come that they may have life, and that they may have it more abundantly. I am the good shepherd. The good shepherd gives His life for the sheep." (John 10:10-11)

A dramatic presentation of typical temptations and pressures to "fit in" that most every young person faces. And many adults as well. Overlaid by the praise song, *Everything.*[26]

Christ truly does provide everything we need to live joyful and contented lives. But how often we allow ourselves to be pulled away by worldly pleasures that threaten to steal our joy, and even to kill and destroy (John 10:10). Pleasures that, to our horror, we cannot later break free from, no matter how hard we try. Pleasures with addictive power that threaten to keep us forever enslaved.

Watch the full 5:46 clip. Then click on it again at the 3:55 mark. The lead character has finally decided that all she wants and needs is Jesus. She has once-and-for-all decided that she wants out. Out of all the addictive substances and behaviors. But the harder she tries to escape, the stronger their hold. Escape is possible only if Jesus, the Good Shepherd, intervenes. And intervene He does, giving His life for her (John 10:11), and taking upon Himself all of the pain and suffering that she deserved.

My "silver bullet" whenever I feel the urge to give in to the flesh. Pull up this app, click on the 3:55 mark, and run to Jesus. It is *impossible* for me to enter this app at the 3:55 mark, and even think about entertaining the lusts of the flesh (Galatians 5:16). Impossible! Thank you, Holy Spirit!

> *It is* impossible *for me to enter this app at the 3:55 mark, and even think about entertaining the lusts of the flesh (Galatians 5:16). Impossible!*

#21 – How He Loves
(John Mark McMillan / Sixsteps)

"For God so loved the world that He gave His only begotten Son, that whoever believes in Him should not perish but have everlasting life." ... And we have known and believed the love that God has for us. God is love, and he who abides in love abides in God, and God in him. (John 3:16 and I John 4:16)

There is something unusually compelling about "hearing" the cardboard testimonies of a group of believers with such widely differing salvation and sanctification stories. No words. Only their silent and succinct cardboard testimonies. Overlaid with the praise song, *How He Loves*.[27] A time for the viewer to pause and reflect on his or her own story. Every viewer can find something in this app to identify with. Something for the Holy Spirit to seize upon and arrest their heart.

> *Every viewer can find something in this app to identify with. Something for the Holy Spirit to seize upon and arrest their heart.*

For the genuinely born-again believer still struggling to fully overcome an addiction, there is no better place to be. So long as he remains sheltered in the Spirit (return the clip to 0:00, and replay as often as needed), he cannot possibly fulfill the lust of the flesh (Galatians 5:16).

#22 – Mary, Did You Know?
(Mark Lowry, Buddy Greene / RCA Records)

"And she will bring forth a Son, and you shall call His name JESUS, for He will save His people from their sins."
(Matthew 1:21)

The first of two apps featuring a mix of touching scenes from Bible-based movies overlaid with an appropriate spiritual song. The video footage is from *Son of God (2014)*, a full-length feature film adaption of the 10-hour television miniseries, *The Bible*. And, of course, *Mary, Did You Know?*[28] is a modern Christmas favorite of many believers.

The special bond that mothers have with their baby boys. May the Holy Spirit use this bond to transform this app into a "silver bullet" for mothers in the reading audience.

#23 – Revelation Song
(Jennie Lee Riddle / INO Records)

And they sang a new song, saying: "You are worthy to take the scroll, and to open its seals; for You were slain, and have redeemed us to God by Your blood ... Worthy is the Lamb who was slain to receive power and riches and wisdom, and strength and honor and glory and blessing!"
(Revelation 5:9, 12)

The second of two apps featuring touching scenes from Bible-based movies overlaid with an appropriate spiritual song. The video footage is created from a mix of three full-length feature films: *The Nativity Story (2006)*, *The Visual Bible: The Gospel of John (2003)*, and *The Passion of the Christ (2004)*. And *Revelation Song*[29] was a *Billboard* No. 1 Hot Christian Song for 11 weeks in 2009.

DIVINE POWER TO DEMOLISH STRONGHOLDS

**For though we walk in the flesh, we do not war according to the flesh. For the weapons of our warfare are not carnal but mighty in God for pulling down strongholds
(II Corinthians 10:3-4)**

Our memory banks store every experience—good and bad—that we have ever had. How sweet to recall that first time I walked into a perfectly manicured major league ballpark, the best-in-class score I had on that killer calculus exam, or a first kiss. Unfortunately, I am also able to recall most sexual temptations I've experienced and how good it felt on those occasions when I yielded to them.

At conversion, the genuinely born-again believer would have all memories of his yielding to sexual temptations forever removed. But there are no magic erase buttons. The old man, with all his pre-conversion baggage, remains. And he will not go quietly. Thus begins, in every believer, to varying degrees, a war between the flesh and the Spirit (Galatians 5:17).

While the born-again believer must still walk in the flesh, he is not to wage this war using fleshly weapons (II Corinthians 10:3). If there is even a hint of the flesh in his weaponry, he should not expect any enemy strongholds to fall.

God has promised a way of escape from every temptation (I Corinthians 10:13). And He has equipped every genuinely born-again believer with mighty spiritual weapons for the pulling down of these enemy strongholds (II Corinthians 10:4). That these weapons are "not carnal, but mighty in God" suggests that the pulldown might even be accomplished relatively quickly.

If I am using God's mighty weapons correctly, I should not be surprised by a dramatic drop in both the number and strength of enemy attacks (see *Real Data*, Chapter 8). Nor should I be surprised that, without help from an accountability partner/group, I am now able to walk away from attacks of the flesh that had previously gotten the better of me (again, see *Real Data*, Chapter 8). If I am a born-again child of God, and if I am relying *solely* on the Holy Spirit, and His power to deliver from the lusts of the flesh (Galatians 5:16), then I have every reason to believe that these strongholds can be pulled down, and likely in much less time than it took me to erect them.

Everyone is wired differently. Numbers and timelines will, therefore, vary from person-to-person. Reductions in the number of enemy attacks, and the timelines required for pulling down enemy strongholds, will be functions of both personal history and level of addiction.[30,31,32]

IN PRAISE OF THE HOLY SPIRIT

The Holy Scriptures tell us much of the character and person of both God, and His Son, the Lord Jesus Christ. But most believers know comparatively little of the character and person of the Holy Spirit. This despite the fact that soon after Jesus ascended into heaven He sent the Holy Spirit to comfort (John 16:7), and to guide believers into all truth (John 16:13). Limited in their understanding of His intended role in their lives, too many believers are failing to fully tap into their primary Power Source, the Holy Spirit. As a result, to both their and the Church's loss, too many are failing to realize anywhere near their full potential as Christians.

It is the Spirit that convicts of sin, and of righteousness, and of judgment to come (John 16:8). But ask a believer what it means to "walk in the Spirit," and most responses will fall well short of the mark. Some believe (as I once did), that they, as born-again believers, are already always walking in the Spirit (see *The Galatians 5:16 Revelation*, Chapter 6). This mistaken belief prevents digging deeper to allow the Holy Spirit to guide the believer into the true meaning and significance of what it means to "walk in the Spirit." Others (as I once did) associate expressions like "walking in the Spirit" with practices specific to the charismatic churches. These too will have their mistaken belief prevent them from digging deeper to allow the Spirit to reveal the true meaning and significance of what it means to "walk in the Spirit."

How unfortunate. In either case, by failing to allow the Holy Spirit to reveal this expression's true meaning and significance, the believer unknowingly relegates the Spirit to a position of lesser importance. Failing to discover this expression's true meaning and significance, the believer unknowingly disables one of the Spirit's more important functions—that of delivering believers from lusts of the flesh (Galatians 5:16).

> *Failing to discover this expression's true meaning and significance, the believer unknowingly disables one of the Spirit's more important functions—that of delivering believers from lusts of the flesh (Galatians 5:16).*

Please understand. I am no more critical of these believers and their mistaken beliefs than I am of myself. I did not "get" the Holy Spirit's role in delivering believers from fleshly lusts (Galatians 5:16) on a first, second, or even a forty-second (42nd) reading! It is hoped that bringing these mistaken beliefs to light will serve as a wake-up call to more in the Church. Echoing the words of Francis Chan, it is my hope and prayer that more will be willing to take a fresh look at familiar passages on the Spirit (e.g., Galatians 5:16, Romans 8:1-4, Romans 8:12-13, Ephesians 3:20-21), to make sure that they have not overlooked anything.[33] As Pastor Chan has so famously stated:

> *... we've ignored the Spirit for far too long, and we are reaping the disastrous results ... (let us) stop and remember the One we've forgotten, the Spirit of the living God.[34]*

For all the comfort (John 16:7), and for all the guidance provided into that which is true (John 16:13), I say to this oft-neglected, oft-misunderstood Third Person in the Trinity, "Thank you, Holy Spirit!"

SIGNATURE OF THE HOLY SPIRIT

I recall the first time that I saw the *P90X*[35] infomercial on late night television (when I still had cable, c. 2008). The rationale for how/why this exercise program worked resonated with me. The muscle confusion discussions made perfect sense. I was only watching an infomercial. It would be another week or so until the DVDs would arrive in the mail. And yet, I already had strong confidence that this was an exercise program that was going to work for me. It made too much exercise science sense not to.

I had a similar experience as the *Way of Escape* Battle Plan began to take shape. Once the connection was made between God's promised way of escape (I Corinthians 10:13), and the discipline (Galatians 5:16) and means (Ephesians 5:18b-19 and the Gaither Homecoming DVDs) of walking in the Spirit, the Spirit Himself quietly assured me that my search for God's promised way of escape was nearing a successful conclusion. The *Way of Escape* Battle Plan (see the two end-of-chapter figures) had the Holy Spirit's signature written all over it. I already had strong confidence that this was a purity program that was going to work for me. It made too much spiritual sense not to.

Dear reader, I hope and pray that, at some point, you have had a similar experience while reading this book. Perhaps you got an inkling that something good was about to happen while reading the "What's New?" in the Author Foreword. Or maybe it was later, in Chapter 6, as the full implications of Galatians 5:16 sank in for possibly the very first time. Or perhaps it was when you played your copy of *Let Freedom Ring*, and discovered that *A Few Good Men*[2] had the same Spirit-filling effect on you as it did The Homecoming Friends during that taping. Whatever the triggering event, I hope and pray that at some point, while reading, you have stopped and thought, "This makes so much spiritual sense. This may just work for me too."

By following the simple steps outlined in Chapters 6-7, in a matter of only a few weeks or months, you should be well on your way to creating a library of flesh-diffusing apps that is uniquely fitted to you, and your unique Spirit-filling triggers. Is this not about the most wonderful news that you could possibly hear, especially if you have ever struggled with sexual sins? While this latest chapter in your quest for sexual purity is only now just beginning, I pray that your hopes for success are already high.

THE "JOHN 3:8ERS"

"The wind blows where it wishes, and you hear the sound of it, but cannot tell where it comes from and where it goes. So is everyone who is born of the Spirit." (John 3:8)

The Holy Spirit will often use emotion-charged images of Spirit-filled fellow believers to escort me into His presence (see KEY INSIGHT, Chapter 6). None are better at capturing these Spirit-filled fellow believers on camera than the Gaither Music Group. Numbered among The Homecoming Friends are many of whom I affectionately refer to as "John 3:8ers" i.e., those believers in whom the influence of the unseen Spirit, like a gale-force wind, is powerfully manifest.

No, the Holy Spirit is not caught on camera during these tapings! But His presence is clearly seen. In the tears of tenderhearted Homecoming Friends Candy Hemphill Christmas[5,8,9,13] and Sheri Easter.[3,7] And in the cannot-stay-seated, fist-pumping cries of Glen Payne.[16,36,37] Not sure where to begin building your library of Spirit-anointed, flesh-diffusing apps? Why not try a few of these "John 3:8ers" from the Homecoming concert series?

SWEET REVENGE

There is a little of what some have termed "sweet revenge"[38] being exacted here. The very medium that the wicked one has used to weaken the born-again believer's witness is now being used to set believers free. In most instances, it was the viewing of pornographic videos that led to the addiction. In the *Way of Escape* Battle Plan, it is again the viewing of videos—but now of the Spirit-anointed kind—that is setting believers free.

Perhaps we should have been looking to video weaponry for a way of escape from porn addiction all along. Advances in brain science seem to indicate that a video antidote is preferred to break free from a video addiction (see *Reprogramming the Brain*, Chapter 2, and the App #14 discussions, earlier here in Chapter 7). And does not a careful reading of I Corinthians 10:13 also suggest that God's promised way of escape would be uniquely fitted to each temptation (see the non-italicized portion of I Corinthians 10:13 below)? At least one other author has made a similar observation.[39]

> *... but **God is faithful, who will not allow you to be tempted beyond what you are able,** but with the temptation will also make the way of escape, that you may be able to bear it (I Corinthians 10:13).*

If *flesh-based videos* are the temptation that led to the addiction, it would be "sweet revenge" for God to use *Spirit-anointed videos* in crafting His way of escape. A video antidote for a video addiction. How perfect! Or, to gain my point, am I guilty of reading too much into Scripture? Let each reader judge for themselves.

BIBLE-BASED

Chapter 1: There is a Promised
Way of Escape (I Corinthians 10:13)

Pre-Emptive Strikes

Chapter 3: Exercising Spiritual Gifts (I Corinthians 12:7)
Chapter 4: Offending Eye Removed (Matthew 5:29)
Chapter 5: Watch and Pray (Matthew 26:41)

Chapter 6: Walking in the Spirit

Walk in the Spirit, and You Shall not Fulfill
the Lust of the Flesh (Galatians 5:16)

Application: When the Flesh Attacks, Run to a Place
Where a Filling of the Spirit is Experienced
… and *Stay There* Until the Danger Passes.

Walking in the Spirit—Six Examples:

1. Read Spirit-Inspired Bible   Words-Only
2. Pray Spirit-Inspired Scripture   (*non*-emotional, *non*-visual)

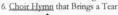

3. Pastor's Heart-Tugging Sermon
4. Missionary's Moving Video   Limbic
5. Drama Team's Touching Skit   (emotional, visual)
6. Choir Hymn that Brings a Tear

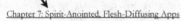

Chapter 7: Spirit-Anointed, Flesh-Diffusing Apps

Homecoming Concert DVDs (Ephesians 5:18b-19)
1441 Tracks, 53 DVDs, 16 Apps
Corporate Worship Atmosphere (all 16 apps)
Worshippers Moved by the Spirit to Tears (apps 1-12)
Spirit-Fired Power Anthems (apps 13-16)

WHAT'S NEW?

1. Ch 2: Emotional/Visual Spiritual Weaponry
2. Ch 6: Walking in the Spirit / Galatians 5:16 Revelation
3. Ch 6: *Active* Pursuit of Regular Relationship Intimacy
   with the Holy Spirit (drop the passivity!)
4. Ch 8: Dramatic Drop in Enemy "Incomings"
5. Ch 6-10: Accountability Partner/Group *not* Required!

NEUROSCIENCE LINK
(Chapter 2)

Brain Plasticity

Cradle-to-Grave, for Better or Worse,
Brain is Constantly Changing & Remolding Itself
(scientific confirmation of Romans 12:2)

Prefrontal Cortex

Brain's Chief Command & Control Center
Place of Higher Reasoning & Impulse Control
(think *non*-emotional, *non*-visual)

Limbic System

Processor of Emotions
Input Receiver for the Senses
Involved in Experiencing Pleasure
Image Imprints Stored in Memory Here
Part of Brain Where Addiction Takes Place
(think emotional, visual)

Words-Only Counterattacks That, for the Addict,
are Largely Ineffective vs. Limbic Attacks
of the Flesh When at Peak Strength

**FOR HEALING TO OCCUR,
THE LIMBIC SYSTEM
MUST BE ACCESSED, AND
THE BRAIN REPROGRAMMED**

Accesses the Limbic System
With the Highly Emotional, Highly Visual
Spiritual Content Needed to Reprogram the Brain

Limbic Weaponry

Healthier Neural Pathways Created & Deepened,
as Unhealthy Neural Pathways are Pruned Back
(neurological principle of use-it-or-lose-it)
(scientific confirmation of James 4:7-8a)

The *Way of Escape* Battle Plan
(full order of battle)

OTHER APPLICATIONS

This work has focused on the Spirit-anointed apps as flesh-diffusers. But might the Spirit—the Comforter (John 16:7)—have additional comforting applications? Other addictions come to mind. Sooner or later, most must grapple with grief resulting from the loss of a loved one. Millions also suffer from chronic pain and associated mood disorders such as depression and anxiety.

Spirit-anointed, *flesh-diffusing* apps are the star of this story. But might Spirit-anointed, *grief-relieving* apps or Spirit-anointed, *depression-combating* apps star in sequels focusing on a more holistic approach to overall wellness? The same apps would star. Only the targeted affliction would change. But I leave this for other author/researchers and another time.

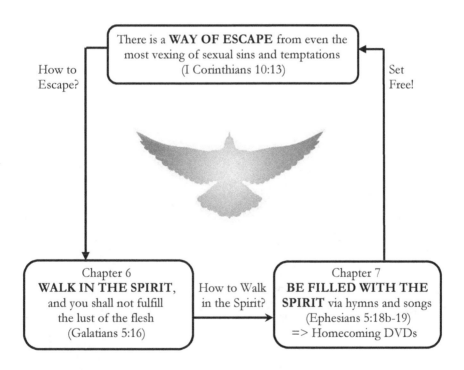

The *Way of Escape* Battle Plan
(key Chapters 6-7 components)

CASE STUDY

**Prove all things; hold fast that which is good
(I Thessalonians 5:21 - KJV).**

The flesh is quiet for now. But knowing that it will eventually attack, a series of pre-emptive strikes are to be launched to keep the flesh in its relatively weakened state:

- Large chunks of once-idle time are to be filled with ministries that make use of spiritual gifts (Chapter 3)
- At home, at the office, and while traveling, all electronic devices that could potentially become a block of stumbling are to be either eliminated or effectively neutralized (Chapter 4)
- The "Watch and Pray" brigade is to be mobilized to aid in avoiding temptation, with special emphasis given to the increased amount of discretionary time available over the weekend (Chapter 5)
- Originally designed as a counterattack weapon, but having proven to be wildly effective in pre-emptive mode, waves of Spirit-anointed, flesh-diffusing apps are

also to be deployed (Chapters 6-7)

HYPOTHETICAL EXAMPLE

For the sake of discussion, I will assume that, on average, the flesh launches 100 attacks on Chris, a single Christian male, over some specified time, T. As each of the four pre-emptive strikes are added to the *Way of Escape* Battle Plan, hypothetical (but still trend-wise correct) data will separately track the impact of each individual strike. The chapter will then close with real data generated while writing this book when the full *Way of Escape* Battle Plan was in place, including all four pre-emptive strike options.

No Pre-Emptive Strikes: Chris is not even aware that God has equipped him with spiritual gifts (Chapter 3). There are several ministries within the local church that would be good fits. But his job wears him out during the week. Chris needs his weekends to recharge, so he has yet to plug in to any ministry at church.

While he no longer frequents bars or strip clubs, the unfiltered Internet still flows freely into Chris' home and onto his smartphone. He cannot conceive of life without the Internet. And adding blocking software (Chapter 4) is too much of a hassle, especially at work. Chris has quit the bar scene. But he still has 24/7 access to a porn store on his laptop and smartphone. He's usually strong. But when bored, stressed, or worn out from work, he will visit a few of his favorite porn sites.

Chris is aware that the increased discretionary time available to him over the weekends makes him more vulnerable to temptation. Still, he rarely ever sets time aside to watch or pray over these times of heightened temptation (Chapter 5).

Chris is excited to read of Galatians 5:16's promised Spirit-led escape from lusts of the flesh. Rightly secure in his salvation, and fully indwelt by the Holy Spirit, he wrongly assumes that he is now already always walking in the Spirit. Thoughts of deploying Spirit-anointed apps (Chapters 6-7) have, therefore, never even crossed his mind.

Chris has entered this battle virtually naked. He has done next-to-nothing to protect against attacks from the flesh. He wonders why he still struggles. And is ashamed every time he fails. Finding comfort in passages like Romans 7:17-25, he wrongly assumes that his inconsistent obedience is normal. Never having intentionally pursued a way of escape, there is little reason to expect that Chris' situation will improve. He has positioned himself to fall far short of his potential as a Christian. He will continue to experience no less than 100 attacks from the flesh over time T (figure below). In truth, if the porn dabbling continues unchecked, addiction will eventually set in. Chris will then need to view sex acts of an increasingly novel and/or hardcore nature to achieve the same sexual high,[1,2,3] and the number of attacks over time T will far exceed 100.

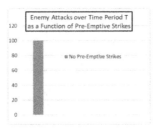

Exercising Spiritual Gifts (Chapter 3): How different is Chris' life once he discovers his spiritual gifts. The free weekends that formerly offered so much temptation are now filled with wholesome Christian-based activities and works of service.

Chris acknowledges that the "too worn out from work" line was an excuse to stay home and look at porn on the weekends. On Fridays, Chris may now be found at his church's Friday Fun Night, a ministry that he helped start by exercising his gift for administration. On Saturdays he taps into his gift for teaching by preparing for the Adult Bible Fellowship (ABF) class he volunteered to co-lead on Sunday mornings.

Chris' weekends are now filled with activities that exercise his spiritual gifts. Now when the flesh calls, it's getting a busy signal. With his spiritual gifts firing on all cylinders, he is now experiencing only 70 attacks from the flesh over time T (figure below).

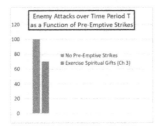

Offending Eye Removed (Chapter 4): Attacks of the flesh are further reduced once Chris removes all magazines and DVDs of a pornographic nature from his home. More reductions follow after Chris installs blocking software on his electronic devices and drops cable TV. The attacks of the flesh are reduced still further when Chris moves his work computer to a location where the monitor can be seen by passersby in the hallway. With his spiritual gifts still firing and his electronic devices under control, Chris is now experiencing only 40 attacks from the flesh over time T (figure below).

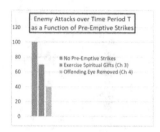

Watch and Pray (Chapter 5): Even with most weekend hours now filled with ministries that exercise his spiritual gifts, Chris still finds that weekend evenings provide opportunities for the flesh to strike. Aware that he is still vulnerable in those hours immediately following Friday Fun Night, he has added a short time of Scripture reading and prayer to the close of the Fun Night festivities. He also makes it a point to always join the group that goes out to eat before heading home. Chris is still prepping on Saturdays for his Sunday morning ABF class. And he continues to maintain control over his electronic devices. Quite remarkably, he is now experiencing only 10 attacks from the flesh over time T (figure below).

Spirit-Anointed Apps (Chapters 6-7): Attacks are down, but Chris is keenly aware that he still too often succumbs to the flesh. But then he saw it. He had read the verse many times before, but this time it stopped him in his tracks. Claiming Galatians 5:16's promise of victory over the flesh, Chris begins building a library of Spirit-anointed apps.

Even while the library is still under construction, he notices that the "incomings" are continuing to fall, both in number and strength. Remarkably, Chris is now only having to endure two (2) much more easily diffused attacks over time T (figure below).

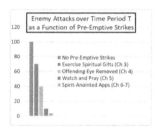

In the example that has gone before, the number of enemy attacks (e.g., 100, 70, 40, 10, 2) over time T are hypothetical. But the trend is not. The number of attacks will most certainly decline with each added pre-emptive strike. To close this chapter, I now share real data, gathered while writing this book.

REAL DATA

The preceding example is largely hypothetical. But not entirely. Portions are loosely based on my own personal experience. The 100, 70, and 40 attacks of the flesh over time T are exaggerated hypothetical numbers. But the final drop, from an estimated 10 to roughly 2 over time T, where T = 1 month, was real.

Dramatic Drop in Incomings: This dramatic drop in "incomings" was the most pleasant of surprises. Regular, near-daily viewing of the Spirit-anointed apps *in pre-emptive mode* was the difference-maker. I had been practicing various forms of the Chapter 3-5 spiritual disciplines my entire Christian life. While these disciplines were essential for spiritual growth, it was not until after I began regularly viewing/screening the Spirit-anointed apps *in pre-emptive mode* that I experienced this dramatic drop in "incomings."

> *Regular, near-daily viewing of the Spirit-anointed apps* **in pre-emptive mode** *was the difference-maker ... it was not until after I began regularly viewing/screening the Spirit-anointed apps* **in pre-emptive mode** *that I experienced this dramatic drop in "incomings."*

Unbeknownst to me at the time, healthier neural pathways were already being created and deepened, even during those hundreds of hours spent screening candidates for inclusion in my library of Spirit-anointed apps (beginning on the 2017 July Fourth Weekend). Strong testimony indeed to the Spirit's inner-working power to deliver believers from lusts of the flesh (Galatians 5:16). The promises of God are true, and never fail (James 4:7-8a). Lord, I believe; help my unbelief (Mark 9:24).

> *Therefore submit to God. Resist the devil and he will flee from you. Draw near to God and He will draw near to you ... (James 4:7-8a)*

Everyone is wired differently. Numbers will, therefore, vary from person-to-person. Other authors have quite reasonably assumed that the number of attacks will be a function of personal history and level of addiction.[4,5,6] Some will experience more than a one-fifth reduction in "incomings," some less. But the amazing promise of James 4:7-8a may be claimed by all. Dear reader, as you plan your way of escape, begin by praying and claiming this wonderful promise of God.

Reduced-Strength Incomings: The Spirit-anointed apps dramatically reduce the number of "incomings." But there is more. They also take the punch out of those remaining less-frequent "incomings" that do still manage to break through.

Once neural pathways were rewired, I found that I could simply walk away from most of these less-frequent, reduced-strength attacks. How ironic. First, the Spirit-anointed apps, originally designed for use as a counterattack weapon, turned out to be wildly effective in pre-emptive mode. And now, when enemy "incomings" did manage to break through, these apps rarely ever even needed to be deployed in counterattack mode. So much for my skills as a weapons designer. But what strong testimony again to the Spirit's inner-working power to deliver believers from the lusts of the flesh (Galatians 5:16).

> *Once neural pathways were rewired, I found that I could simply walk away from most of these less-frequent, reduced-strength attacks.*

Complete Mind Renewal: But His blessings did not stop here. Complete mind renewal was also achieved. Definitions vary, but mine is captured in another author's four-word catch phrase summarizing ownership rights of that certain member of the male believer's body: God-Wife-Me-Pee.[7]

I am not my own. I have been bought with a price, the precious shed blood of Jesus Christ. God is, therefore, the first owner (I Corinthians 6:19-20). If I were to marry, my wife would be the second owner. I am the third owner. But I have urinating rights only. To have gotten to this place in my Christian walk, my mind had to first be completely renewed.

Praise the Holy Spirit: As the full manuscript heads off to the publisher (January 2022), this sexually healthy, single Christian male has not "acted out" sexually for 100% of days over the most recent 34 months! Yet again, all credit and praise to the Holy Spirit, and His inner-working power to deliver believers from lusts of the flesh (Galatians 5:16).

It is surprisingly easy to walk uprightly when the Holy Spirit is in the lead. Easier than I ever could have asked or thought (Ephesians 3:20). Thank you, Holy Spirit!

> *Now to Him who is able to do exceedingly abundantly above all that we ask or think, according to the power that works in us, To Him be glory in the church by Christ Jesus to all generations, forever and ever. Amen (Ephesians 3:20-21).*

Continuing Research: Data reported herein is for a one-person Case Study. A larger sample size is needed. It is hoped that others can take this fertile area of research to the next level to confirm this work's major claim: For a non-trivial percentage of men in the Church, mind renewal is possible without the aid of an accountability partner or group. These men may need to do nothing more than learn how to step up the degree to which they walk in the Spirit (Galatians 5:16). These men may need to do nothing more than drop the passivity, and learn how to actively pursue more regular relationship intimacy with the Holy Spirit (see KEY REGULARITY, Chapter 6).

> *The Major Claim of this Work: For a non-trivial percentage of men in the Church, mind renewal is possible without the aid of an accountability partner or group.*

But as these larger clinical studies proceed, let us be ever-careful not to underestimate the power of the Holy Spirit. Let us be ever-mindful that Scripture places no limitations on the efficacy of the Holy Spirit to deliver believers from lusts of the flesh (e.g., Galatians 5:16, Romans 8:1-4, Romans 8:12-13, Ephesians 3:20-21). Deliverance is not limited to only the lightly afflicted. Or to only those with solid Christian upbringings. Scripturally speaking, the playing field is level. It may take a little longer for some, but to *all* who choose to "walk in the Spirit," God has promised deliverance from *all* lusts of the flesh (Galatians 5:16).

> *I say then: Walk in the Spirit, and you shall not fulfill the lust of the flesh (Galatians 5:16).*

Ready to try the *Way of Escape* Battle Plan for yourself? Appendix F describes the Escape Plan in five easy steps.

For biblical, neurological, and non-technical explanations of why "walking in the Spirit" works, see Appendix G.

MIND RENEWAL OPTIONS

And do not be conformed to this world, but be transformed by the renewing of your mind, that you may prove what is that good and acceptable and perfect will of God (Romans 12:2).

In the inner man of every born-again believer, there is an ongoing battle between the flesh and the Spirit (Galatians 5:17). For many, the Spirit reigns, with only occasional setbacks. But for those still struggling to fully overcome a porn/sex addiction, the flesh is posting wins in this battle far too often.

The literature describes a variety of plans for overcoming a porn/sex addiction. Broken down, these plans all fall into one of two camps: Flesh-Starvers or Spirit-Feeders. Component parts of these plans often borrow from the other camp. But broadly speaking, every battle plan for purity may be classified as either a Flesh-Starver or a Spirit-Feeder.

ACCOUNTABILITY-BASED PURITY PROGRAMS: STARVING THE FLESH

Component parts of accountability-based purity programs do indeed include examples of feeding of the Spirit. The Spirit-inspired Scriptures are quoted throughout. And other Spirit-edifying activities are encouraged. But broadly speaking, programs that depend on weekly check-ups with other *fellow strugglers* to help win the battle against the flesh cannot be classified as Spirit-Feeders. Such programs are rightly classified as Flesh-Starvers.

THE *WAY OF ESCAPE* BATTLE PLAN: FEEDING THE SPIRIT

Component parts of the *Way of Escape* Battle Plan do indeed call for a starving of the flesh. The disciplines described in Chapters 4-5 are prime examples. But broadly speaking, a Battle Plan where the *Holy Spirit* is the only Person called upon to help win the battle against the flesh is rightly classified as a Spirit-Feeder.

Many have overcome a porn/sex addiction with the help of an accountability-based purity program. But healing is not the exclusive domain of accountability partners/groups. As described herein, the still-struggling may need to do nothing more than learn how to step up the degree to which they walk in the Spirit (Galatians 5:16). The still-struggling may need to do nothing more than drop the passivity, and learn how to actively pursue more regular relationship intimacy with the Holy Spirit (see KEY REGULARITY, Chapter 6).

> *Healing is not the exclusive domain of accountability partners/groups.*

The *Way of Escape* Battle Plan offers a fundamentally different approach to mind renewal. Fundamentally different than any approach currently being discussed in the Christian literature. All purity programs rightly pay homage to the Holy Spirit. But none that I am aware of provide a step-by-step "how-to" procedure for experiencing the Spirit's filling. Nor do any explain how regularly repeating that Spirit-filling experience eventually leads to a renewing of the mind.

The *Way of Escape* Battle Plan goes the extra mile. Or two. It provides a step-by-step "how-to" procedure for experiencing a filling of the Spirit (see my App #7 closing paragraph; readers interested in trying the *Way of Escape* Battle Plan will replicate my procedure, substituting their apps for mine). The Case Study then goes on to show how regularly repeating that Spirit-filling experience eventually leads to a renewing of the mind (see *Real Data*, Chapter 8).

DUAL APPROACHES

Some may simply prefer the support and camaraderie that groups provide (Galatians 6:1-2, James 5:16). These individuals can still realize the benefits of the *Way of Escape* Battle Plan. The Spirit-anointed apps can be seamlessly incorporated into any accountability-based purity program. Apps that issue in a filling of the Spirit only improve the odds of victory over the flesh and should be a welcome addition to every believer's arsenal of weapons.

Others, having had their minds renewed, may still wish to be part of an accountability group for the extra layer of protection it provides. Each will have to tailor their Battle Plan to fit their unique situation.

Whether it is via an accountability partner/group, with the use of Spirit-anointed apps—or by some combination of the two—so long as the limbic system is accessed and the brain is reprogrammed, healing will occur (see *Reprogramming the Brain*, Chapter 2).

> *Whether it is via an accountability partner/group, with the use of Spirit-anointed apps—or by some combination of the two—so long as the limbic system is accessed and the brain is reprogrammed, healing will occur.*

FRESH HOPE FOR THE STILL-STRUGGLING

Now may the God of hope fill you with all joy and peace in believing, that you may abound in hope by the power of the Holy Spirit (Romans 15:13).

REDUCED NUMBER AND STRENGTH OF INCOMINGS

This work has demonstrated that regular, near-daily viewing of the Spirit-anointed, flesh-diffusing apps rewires neural pathways, which, in turn, significantly reduces both the number and strength of enemy "incomings." While numbers will vary from person-to-person, in the Case Study reported herein, these reduced-strength attacks of the flesh occurred only about one-fifth as often, once cleaner neural pathways were established. Given the choice, it is certain that every individual struggling with sexual sins would elect to deal with roughly two (2) reduced-strength attacks of the flesh per month, rather than a steady barrage of higher-strength "incomings" at the 5X rate of 10 attacks per month (for the backstory on these numbers, see *Real Data*, Chapter 8).

COMPLETE MIND RENEWAL

In the Case Study reported herein, complete mind renewal was also achieved. But all Christian authors and purity programs that I have reviewed insist that this is a battle that cannot be won alone. So how could complete mind renewal have been achieved without the help of an accountability partner or group?

Crucial to achieving mind renewal without accountability is to first realize that we are not in this battle alone. All genuinely born-again believers are fully indwelt by the Holy Spirit at conversion. For the still-struggling, mind renewal without accountability may require doing nothing more than learning how to step up the degree to which they walk in the Spirit (Galatians 5:16). For the still-struggling, mind renewal without accountability may require doing nothing more than dropping the passivity, and learning how to actively pursue more regular relationship intimacy with the Holy Spirit (see KEY REGULARITY, Chapter 6).

ACCOUNTABILITY PARTNER/GROUP NOT REQUIRED

Finally, and most significantly, the *Way of Escape* Battle Plan enables complete mind renewal without ever having to enlist the aid of an accountability partner or group. The *Way of Escape* Battle Plan relies solely on the Holy Spirit's power to deliver believers from lusts of the flesh (Galatians 5:16). The still-struggling now have another option. The still-struggling now have fresh hope for discovering that long-sought-after way of escape (I Corinthians 10:13). A way that does not require enlisting the aid of an accountability partner or group.

THANK YOU, HOLY SPIRIT!

CREDITS

REFERENCES

Author Foreword
1. Wiles, J., and T. Wiles, *Conquer Series: The Battle Plan for Purity (Study Guide, Volume 1)*, Second Printing, KingdomWorks Studios, Stuart, FL, page 21, 2017
2. *Ibid.*, page 9
3. Wiles, J., and T. Wiles, *Conquer Series: The Battle Plan for Purity (Study Guide, Volume 2)*, First Printing, KingdomWorks Studios, Stuart, FL, page 33, 2017
4. Wiles, J., and T. Wiles, *Conquer Series: The Battle Plan for Purity (12-disc DVD set)*, Volume 2, Disc 2, Track 2 – Tools to Conquer, KingdomWorks Studios, Stuart, FL, 2017

Chapter 1: Introduction
1. Wiles, J., and T. Wiles, *Conquer Series: The Battle Plan for Purity (Study Guide, Volume 1)*, Second Printing, KingdomWorks Studios, Stuart, FL, page 9, 2017
2. *Ibid.*, page 21
3. Lewis, C.L., *Matthew Fontaine Maury: The Pathfinder of the Seas*, First Printing, United States Naval Institute, Annapolis, MD, 1927
4. Wiles, J., and T. Wiles, *Conquer Series: The Battle Plan for Purity (Study*

Guide, Volume 1), Second Printing, KingdomWorks Studios, Stuart, FL, pages 32, 42, and 52, 2017

Chapter 2: The Neurology of Addiction

1. Doidge, N., *The Brain That Changes Itself: Stories of Personal Triumph from the Frontiers of Brain Science*, First Printing, Penguin Books, New York, NY, page xvii, 2007

2. https://en.wikipedia.org/wiki/This_Is_Your_Brain_on_Drugs, accessed August 15, 2017

3. Wiles, J., and T. Wiles, *Conquer Series: The Battle Plan for Purity (12-disc DVD set)*, Volume 1, Disc 4, Track 4 – The Addicted Brain, KingdomWorks Studios, Stuart, FL, 2017

4. Doidge, N., *The Brain That Changes Itself: Stories of Personal Triumph from the Frontiers of Brain Science*, First Printing, Penguin Books, New York, NY, page 383, 2007

5. Wilson, G., *Your Brain on Porn: Internet Pornography and the Emerging Science of Addiction*, First Printing, Commonwealth Publishing, UK, pages 58 and 69, 2014

6. Gross, C., and S. Luff, *Pure Eyes: A Man's Guide to Sexual Integrity*, First Printing, Baker Books, Grand Rapids, MI, pages 83-84, 2010

7. Wilson, G., *Your Brain on Porn: Internet Pornography and the Emerging Science of Addiction*, First Printing, Commonwealth Publishing, UK, pages 36-43, 2014

8. Maltz, W., and L. Maltz, *The Porn Trap: The Essential Guide to Overcoming Problems Caused by Pornography*, First Printing, HarperCollins Publishers, New York, NY, pages 93-94, 2008

9. Struthers, W.M., *Wired for Intimacy: How Pornography Hijacks the Male Brain*, First Printing, InterVarsity Press, Downers Grove, IL, pages 33-36, 2009

10. Wiles, J., and T. Wiles, *Conquer Series: The Battle Plan for Purity (Study Guide, Volume 2)*, First Printing, KingdomWorks Studios, Stuart, FL, page 33, 2017

11. Wiles, J., and T. Wiles, *Conquer Series: The Battle Plan for Purity (12-disc DVD set)*, Volume 2, Disc 2, Track 2 – Tools to Conquer, KingdomWorks Studios, Stuart, FL, 2017

Chapter 3: Identify and Exercise Spiritual Gifts

1. Wagner, C.P., *Your Spiritual Gifts Can Help Your Church Grow*, Fourth Printing, Regal Books from Gospel Light Publishers, Ventura, CA, pages 22 and 26, 2012

2. *Ibid.*, pages 267-274

3. The 21 Spiritual Gifts and How to Grow Them, http://giftstest.com (in partnership with beliefnet)

4. Graf, W., *100 Reasons to Believe the Bible is the Word of God*, Fifth Printing, Createspace, 2018

5. Wagner, C.P., *Your Spiritual Gifts Can Help Your Church Grow*, Fourth Printing, Regal Books from Gospel Light Publishers, Ventura, CA, pages 245-265, 2012

Chapter 4: The Offending Eye Removed

1. *CovenantEyes*, https://covenanteyes.com

Chapter 5: Watch and Pray

1. Wilson, G., *Your Brain on Porn: Internet Pornography and the Emerging Science of Addiction*, First Printing, Commonwealth Publishing, UK, page 59, 2014

Chapter 6: Walking in the Spirit

1. Platt, D., and T. Merida (Series Editors D. Platt, D.L. Akin, and T. Merida), *Christ-Centered Exposition: Exalting Jesus in Galatians*, First Printing, B&H Publishing Group, Nashville, TN, pages 108-109, 2014

2. Barker, K.L., and J.R. Kohlenberger III, *The Expositor's Bible Commentary—Abridged Edition: New Testament*, First Printing, Zondervan, Grand Rapids, MI, page 739, 1994

3. MacArthur, J., *The MacArthur New Testament Commentary: Galatians*, First Printing, Moody Publishers, Chicago, IL, pages 152-154, 1987

4. Gaither, B., *It's More Than the Music: Life Lessons on Friends, Faith, and What Matters Most*, First Printing, Warner Faith (a division of AOL Time Warner Book Group), pages 1-21, 2003

5. Silvey, J., (Word Music, Big Ole Hit Music, Curb Songs), *Except for Grace*, Track #19 on *Good News (DVD)*, Spring House Productions, Inc., Manufactured by Gaither Music Group, Alexandria, IN, 2000

Chapter 7: Spirit-Anointed, Flesh-Diffusing Applications

1. Green, S., *People Need the Lord (CD)*, The Sparrow Corporation, Brentwood, TN, 1994

2. Jennings, S., and B. Jennings (Townsend and Warbucks Music), *A Few Good Men*, Track #19 on *Let Freedom Ring (DVD)*, Spring House Productions, Inc., Manufactured by Gaither Music Group, Alexandria, IN, 2002

3. Gaither, W.J., G. Gaither, and C. Christian (Gaither Music Company, Inc., Home Sweet Home Music), *Then Came the Morning*, Track #29 on *Whispering Hope (DVD)*, Spring House Productions, Inc., Manufactured by Gaither Music Group, Alexandria, IN, 2000

4. Gaither, W.J., and G. Gaither (Gaither Music Company, Inc.), *Worthy the Lamb*, Track #23 on *South African Homecoming (DVD)*, Spring House Productions, Inc., Manufactured by Gaither Music Group, Alexandria, IN, 2007

5. Gaither, W.J., and G. Gaither (Gaither Music Company, Inc.), *The Old Rugged Cross Made the Difference*, Track #21 on *London Homecoming (DVD)*, Spring House Productions, Inc., Manufactured by Gaither

Music Group, Alexandria, IN, 2001

6. Gaither, W.J., *Rex Nelon Tribute*, Track #20 on *London Homecoming (DVD)*, Spring House Productions, Inc., Manufactured by Gaither Music Group, Alexandria, IN, 2001

7. Wilburn, C.A., and R. Wilburn (Winkin' Music, Darby Corner Music, House of Aaron Music), *Four Days Late*, Track #25 on *I'll Fly Away (DVD)*, Spring House Productions, Inc., Manufactured by Gaither Music Group, Alexandria, IN, 2002

8. Silvey, J., (Word Music, Big Ole Hit Music, Curb Songs), *Except for Grace*, Track #19 on *Good News (DVD)*, Spring House Productions, Inc., Manufactured by Gaither Music Group, Alexandria, IN, 2000

9. Ewing, J. (Landy Ewing Publishing), *He Saw Me*, Track #17 on *Rivers of Joy (DVD)*, Spring House Productions, Inc., Manufactured by Gaither Music Group, Alexandria, IN, 1998

10. Waterman, A.W. (Gaither Vocal Band arrangers, Gaither Music Company), *Yes, I Know*, Track #25 on *Feelin' at Home (DVD)*, Spring House Productions, Inc., Manufactured by Gaither Music Group, Alexandria, IN, 1997

11. Sumner, D., and D. Friend (Gospel Quartet Music), *The Night Before Easter*, Track #21 on *Joy in the Camp (DVD)*, Spring House Productions, Inc., Manufactured by Gaither Music Company, Alexandria, IN, 1997

12. Sumner, D., *Testimony*, Track #19 on *Joy in the Camp (DVD)*, Spring House Productions, Inc., Manufactured by Gaither Music Company, Alexandria, IN, 1997

13. Hemphill, J. (Family and Friends Music, Hemphill Music Company), *Master of the Wind*, Track #20 on *Joy in the Camp (DVD)*, Spring House Productions, Inc., Manufactured by Gaither Music Company, Alexandria, IN, 1997

14. Paschal, J. (Maplesong Music, BMM Music), *Another Soldier's Coming Home*, Track #21 on *Marching to Zion (DVD)*, Spring House Productions, Inc., Manufactured by Gaither Music Group, Alexandria, IN, 1998

15. Paschal, J. (Maplesong Music, BMM Music), *Another Soldier's Coming Home*, Track #9 on *The Best of Janet Paschal from the Homecoming Series (DVD)*, Spring House Productions, Inc., Manufactured by Gaither Music Group, Alexandria, IN, 2007

16. Thomas, D. (McSpadden Music), *I Am Not Ashamed*, Track #12 on *All Day Singin' and Dinner on the Ground (DVD)*, Spring House Productions, Inc., Manufactured by Gaither Music Group, Alexandria, IN, 1995

17. Thomas, D. (McSpadden Music), *I Am Not Ashamed*, Track #5 on *The Best of Janet Paschal from the Homecoming Series (DVD)*, Spring House

Productions, Inc., Manufactured by Gaither Music Group, Alexandria, IN, 2007

18. Crabb, G.D. (Crabb's Song Music), *Through the Fire*, Track #25 on *New Orleans Homecoming (DVD)*, Spring House Productions, Inc., Manufactured by Gaither Music Group, Alexandria, IN, 2002

19. Francisco, D. (New Spring Publishing, Inc.), *He's Alive*, Track #24 on *Tent Revival Homecoming (DVD)*, Spring House Productions, Inc., Manufactured by Gaither Music Group, Alexandria, IN, 2011

20. *I Can Only Imagine: Ultimate Power Anthems of the Christian Faith (CD)*, INO Records, Brentwood, TN, 2004

21. Gaither, G., and W.J. Gaither (Gaither Music Company, Inc.), *Let Freedom Ring*, Track #28 on *Let Freedom Ring (DVD)*, Spring House Productions, Inc., Manufactured by Gaither Music Group, Alexandria, IN, 2002

22. Gaither, G., W.J. Gaither, and D. Daniels (Gaither Music Company, Inc., Ariose Music), *I've Just Seen Jesus*, Track #40 on *Kennedy Center Homecoming (DVD)*, Spring House Productions, Inc., Manufactured by Gaither Music Group, Alexandria, IN, 1999

23. Peterson, A., and B. Shive, *Is He Worthy?*, West Coast Baptist College, https://www.youtube.com/watch?v=qkpUlxGCOtM, 2020

24. Fielding, B., and B. Ligertwood, *What a Beautiful Name*, Hillsong Worship, https://www.youtube.com/watch?v=nQWFzMvCfLE, 2016

25. Gayle, C., R. Kennedy, S. Musso, D. Gentiles, and B. McCleery, *Thank You Jesus for the Blood*, video footage provided by Charity Gayle, https://www.youtube.com/watch?v=dhU-Omwg2rU, 2021

26. Wade, J., *Everything*, video footage from Vineyard Church, https://www.youtube.com/watch?v=u-tb6AOuiDg, 2019

27. McMillan, J.M., *How He Loves*, video footage from Hillside Church, https://www.youtube.com/watch?v=RvDDc5RB6FQ, 2008

28. Lowry, M., and B. Greene, *Mary, Did You Know?*, video footage from *Son of God*, a movie adaption of the 10-part miniseries *The Bible*, https://www.youtube.com/watch?v=ghrkDTbZAa0, 2017

29. Riddle, J.L., *Revelation Song*, video footage from *The Nativity Story*, *The Visual Bible: The Gospel of John*, and *The Passion of the Christ*, https://www.youtube.com/watch?v=S3LK3wlHnVE, 2010

30. Skinner, K.B., *Treating Pornography Addiction: The Essential Tools for Recovery*, First Printing, K. Skinner Corp., Lindon, UT, pages 24-33, 2005

31. Gross, C., and S. Luff, *Pure Eyes: A Man's Guide to Sexual Integrity*, First Printing, Baker Books, Grand Rapids, MI, page 88, 2010

32. Gallagher, S., *At the Altar of Sexual Idolatry*, Third Printing, Pure Life Ministries, Dry Ridge, KY, pages 123-124, 2007

33. Chan, F., *Forgotten God: Reversing Our Tragic Neglect of the Holy Spirit*, First Printing, David C Cook, Colorado Springs, CO, pages 46-47, 2009

34. *Ibid.* (excerpt from the book's online *Amazon* blurb)

35. *P90X: Extreme Home Fitness with Tony Horton (DVD)*, Beachbody, Beverly Hills, CA, 2007

36. Lister, M. (Lillenas Publishing Company), *Where No One Stands Alone*, Track #16 on *Something Beautiful (DVD)*, Spring House Productions, Inc., Manufactured by Gaither Music Group, Alexandria, IN, 1996

37. Gaither, G., W.J. Gaither, and M. Humphries (Gaither Music Company, Writer's Group, Inc.), *Sinner Saved by Grace*, Track #22 on *Joy in the Camp (DVD)*, Spring House Productions, Inc., Manufactured by Gaither Music Company, Alexandria, IN, 1997

38. Wiles, J., and T. Wiles, *Conquer Series: The Battle Plan for Purity (Study Guide, Volume 2)*, First Printing, KingdomWorks Studios, Stuart, FL, page 57, 2017

39. Challies, T., *Sexual Detox: A Guide for Men Who Are Sick of Porn*, First Printing, Cruciform Press, Adelphi, MD, page 105 (text of an 1883 sermon by Charles Spurgeon), 2010

Chapter 8: Case Study

1. Gross, C., and S. Luff, *Pure Eyes: A Man's Guide to Sexual Integrity*, First Printing, Baker Books, Grand Rapids, MI, pages 83-84, 2010

2. Wilson, G., *Your Brain on Porn: Internet Pornography and the Emerging Science of Addiction*, First Printing, Commonwealth Publishing, UK, pages 36-43, 2014

3. Maltz, W., and L. Maltz, *The Porn Trap: The Essential Guide to Overcoming Problems Caused by Pornography*, First Printing, HarperCollins Publishers, New York, NY, pages 93-94, 2008

4. Skinner, K.B., *Treating Pornography Addiction: The Essential Tools for Recovery*, First Printing, K. Skinner Corp., Lindon, UT, pages 24-33, 2005

5. Gross, C., and S. Luff, *Pure Eyes: A Man's Guide to Sexual Integrity*, First Printing, Baker Books, Grand Rapids, MI, page 88, 2010

6. Gallagher, S., *At the Altar of Sexual Idolatry*, Third Printing, Pure Life Ministries, Dry Ridge, KY, pages 123-124, 2007

7. Weiss, D., *Clean: A Proven Plan for Men Committed to Sexual Integrity*, First Printing, Thomas Nelson, Nashville, TN, pages 132-133, 2013

Appendix B: Praying the Promises of God

1. *Matthew Henry's Commentary on the Whole Bible (Volume 1, Genesis to Deuteronomy)*, First Printing, Hendrickson Publishers, Peabody MA, page 155, 1991

2. Arterburn, S., F. Stoeker, and M. Yorkey, *Every Man's Battle: Winning the War on Sexual Temptation One Victory at a Time*, First Printing,

WaterBrook Press (a division of Penguin Random House LLC), New York, NY, pages 44-48, 2000

Appendix C: For the 83 Percent

1. *The Porn Phenomenon: The Impact of Pornography in the Digital Age*, Barna Group, Ventura, CA, page 112, 2016 (83% determined as the average of 79% for Teens and Young Adults and 87% for Adults Age 25 and Older)

2. *Conquer Series: The Battle Plan for Purity* (the 2 million men statistic is reported on their Home Page at https://www.conquerseries.com/)

Appendix D: Why Aren't Others Teaching Spirit-Led Escape from Those Hard-to-Eradicate Lingering Sins?

1. Stanley, C., *Walking in the Holy Spirit*, In Touch Ministries (https://youtube.com/watch?v=r-9L2-aVR4I at the 22:18 mark—but please watch this spot-on sermon in its entirety), 2015

2. Chan, F., *Forgotten God: Reversing Our Tragic Neglect of the Holy Spirit*, First Printing, David C Cook, Colorado Springs, CO, page 75, 2009

3. MacArthur, J., *The MacArthur New Testament Commentary: Romans 1-8*, First Printing, Moody Publishers, Chicago, IL, pages 411-412, 1991

4. MacArthur, J., *The MacArthur New Testament Commentary: Galatians*, First Printing, Moody Publishers, Chicago, IL, page 152, 1987

Appendix E: My Library of Gaither Homecoming Concert DVDs

1. http://www.waynecountry.net/BGH/Gaither.html

2. *Tent Revival (DVD)*, Spring House Productions, Inc., Manufactured by Gaither Music Group, Alexandria, IN, 2011

3. *The Best of Janet Paschal from the Homecoming Series (DVD)*, Spring House Productions, Inc., Manufactured by Gaither Music Group, Alexandria, IN, 2007

4. *Let Freedom Ring (DVD)*, Spring House Productions, Inc., Manufactured by Gaither Music Group, Alexandria, IN, 2002

5. *Good News (DVD)*, Spring House Productions, Inc., Manufactured by Gaither Music Group, Alexandria, IN, 2000

Appendix G: Why "Walking in the Spirit" Works

1. Doidge, N., *The Brain That Changes Itself: Stories of Personal Triumph from the Frontiers of Brain Science*, First Printing, Penguin Books, New York, NY, page 170, 2007

2. Lister, M. (Lillenas Publishing Company), *Where No One Stands Alone*, Track #16 on *Something Beautiful (DVD)*, Spring House Productions, Inc., Manufactured by Gaither Music Group, Alexandria, IN, 1996

3. Lister, M., *Narrative*, Track #17 on *Something Beautiful (DVD)*, Spring House Productions, Inc., Manufactured by Gaither Music Group, Alexandria, IN, 1996

Appendix H: What Must I Do to Be Saved?

1. Arterburn, S., F. Stoeker, and M. Yorkey, *Every Man's Battle: Winning the War on Sexual Temptation One Victory at a Time*, First Printing, WaterBrook Press (a division of Penguin Random House LLC), New York, NY, pages 44-48, 2000

IMAGES

All photographs and illustrations have been reproduced in good faith, recognizing copyrights where required, and always citing the original source.

Bigstock (public domain): 34, 78, 82, 90, 92, 100

Pixabay (public domain): All "Holy Spirit dove" images, 37, 106

Wikimedia Commons (public domain): 178

Wiley Graf: 108, 109, 113-115 (Excel), 168, 170, 172, 174, 176

ESSENTIAL EXTRABIBLICAL READING

1.   Chan, F., *Forgotten God: Reversing Our Tragic Neglect of the Holy Spirit*, First Printing, David C Cook, Colorado Springs, CO, 2009

BATTLE PLANS FOR OTHER FAMILY STRUCTURES

… choose for yourselves this day whom you will serve … But as for me and my house, we will serve the Lord (Joshua 24:15).

Throughout the text, I describe the *Way of Escape* Battle Plan for a single male with no children in the home—a home that has neither an Internet nor a cable TV connection (Family Structure #1). This chapter summarizes that plan in both tabular and text format. Modifications will be required for families that include either a spouse or children (Family Structure #2). The table provides a third (blank) column to be filled in by the interested reader.

Each reader will have to tailor their Battle Plan to fit their unique situation. This is not only about the reader's personal integrity but also that of his entire family. Each will have to develop a plan that works best for both them *and* their house. A plan that gives *each* family member the best opportunity to subdue the flesh, and best serve the Lord (Joshua 24:15).

CH	Description	Family Structure		
		1	2	3
3	Identify & Exercise Spiritual Gifts	√	√	
	No Exercising of Spiritual Gifts			
4	Electronic Devices in the Home			
	Laptop			
	Internet-Connected, Unprotected			
	Internet-Connected, with Accountability/Blocking Software		√	
	No Internet Connection	√		
	Smartphone			
	Internet-Connected, Unprotected			
	Internet-Connected, with Accountability/Blocking Software		√	
	No Internet Connection	√		
	Cable Television			
	Including "Premium" Channels			
	Standard Cable Only		√	
	No Cable Connection	√		
	DVD Player			
	Linked Through Television Display Monitor	√	√	
	Stand-Alone (no TV) with Built-In Display Monitor	√	√	
	No DVD Player			
	Electronic Devices in the Office			
	Laptop or Personal Computer			
	Internet-Connected, Unprotected			
	Internet-Connected, with Accountability/Blocking Software	√	√	
	No Internet Connection			
	Safeguards			
	Hallway-Facing Monitor	√	√	
	See-Through Windows	√	√	
	Desktop Folder of Spirit-Anointed Flesh-Diffusing Apps	√	√	
	Never Alone	√	√	
	No Safeguards			
	Electronic Devices in the Hotel Room			
	Laptop			
	Include in Luggage, Unprotected			
	Include in Luggage, with Accountability/Blocking Software		√	
	No Laptop	√		
	Smartphone			
	Include in Luggage, Unprotected (but room is off-limits)	√		
	Include in Luggage, with Accountability/Blocking Software		√	
	No Smartphone			
	Cable Television			
	Including "Premium" Channels			
	Standard Cable Only			
	No Cable Connection	√	√	
	DVD Player and DVDs Containing Most Powerful Apps			
	Include in Luggage	√	√	
	No DVD Player or DVDs			
5	Watch & Pray			
	Avoid Predictable Attacks	√	√	
	Diffuse Surprise Attacks (apps playing in pre-emptive mode)	√	√	
	Pray to *Avoid* Temptation (Appendix B)	√	√	
	No Watch			
7	Spirit-Anointed, Flesh-Diffusing Applications			

	Sermon Snippets			
	Music/Songs			
	Homecoming Music Videos (pre-emptive mode)	√	√	
	Homecoming Music Videos (counterattack mode)	√	√	
	Choir/Drama/Movie Overlaid w/Song (pre-emptive mode)	√	√	
	Choir/Drama/Movie Overlaid w/Song (counterattack mode)	√	√	
	Other		√	
	No Apps			
6-10	Accountability Partners			
	Enlist Aid of a Trusted Accountability Partner			
	Join an Accountability Group			
	No Accountability Partner/Group	√		

Family Structures:
   1: Wiley Graf, a Single Male with No Children Living in the Home, and Neither Internet nor Cable TV Connection
   2: Multi-Person Home with Internet and Cable TV Connection
   3: Blank (to be filled in by the reader for his unique situation)

Family Structure #1 – Wiley Graf, a Single Male with No Children Living in the Home. No Internet or Cable TV Connection:

Identify and Exercise Spiritual Gifts (Chapter 3): God has equipped every born-again believer with at least one spiritual gift. No exceptions, across all family structures, all should identify and use their gift(s) to glorify God, and to edify His Church.

The Offending Eye Removed (Chapter 4): I choose to be free from the Internet and cable TV in both the home and while traveling. Safeguards, including accountability/blocking software, are recommended for those working in an office environment.

Watch and Pray (Chapter 5): At a first and most fundamental level of "watching," I make a conscious effort to avoid those more predictable situations that have caused me to stumble in the past. I am also careful to set aside 30-60 minutes most evenings to view favorite Spirit-anointed apps in pre-emptive mode that I might take full advantage of the Holy Spirit's power to diffuse "surprise" attacks of the flesh (see Appendix E for four sample playlists). I periodically review/memorize key Scripture passages that promise temptation avoidance and escape, usually closing with some form of *A Prayer for Sexual Purity* (see *Appendix* B).

Spirit-Anointed, Flesh-Diffusing Apps (Chapter 7): My 23 Spirit-anointed, flesh-diffusing apps are used primarily as an offensive weapon in pre-emptive mode. I keep my mind renewed by regularly viewing these apps for 30-60 minutes most evenings (again, see Appendix E for sample playlists).

Accountability Partners (Chapters 6-10): Not needed. My mind has been renewed without the aid of an accountability partner/group. I rely solely on the Holy Spirit's power to deliver me from the lusts of the flesh (Galatians 5:16).

Family Structure #2 – A Multi-Person Home with both an Internet and Cable TV Connection:

Identify and Exercise Spiritual Gifts (Chapter 3): Unchanged from Family Structure #1. Across all family structures, all should identify and use their gift(s) to glorify God, and to edify His Church.

The Offending Eye Removed (Chapter 4)

Electronic Devices in the Home: For the man with a wife or children that regularly access the Internet, "Internet-Connected, with Accountability/Blocking Software" in the home would be a better option for all laptops and smartphones. To head off a civil war, it is assumed that standard cable TV is also back in the home.

Electronic Devices in the Office: Marriage and family do not remove workplace temptations. Office laptops and personal computers should still be equipped with accountability/blocking software, with all recommended safeguards still in place.

Electronic Devices in the Hotel Room: With all electronic devices now "Internet- Connected with

Accountability/Blocking Software," laptops and smartphones may now be safely used in the hotel room. When traveling alone, however, the cable TV connection should still be disabled. A small DVD player and DVDs featuring the most powerful apps should also be included in one's luggage.

Watch and Pray (Chapter 5): Unchanged from Family Structure #1. Marriage and family do not change the fact that believers must remain diligent to watch and pray if they are to break and stay free of sexual addictions.

Spirit-Anointed, Flesh-Diffusing Apps (Chapter 7): Marriage and family do not change the fact that believers must keep neural pathways clean if they are to break and stay free of sexual addictions. Across all family structures, all should be feeding on a steady diet of Spirit-anointed, flesh-diffusing apps in both pre-emptive and counterattack mode. No person will have a library of apps identical to my 23. But there will likely be at least some overlap. Family Structure #2's library will also likely include apps taken from entirely different sources (= "Other" in the table).

Accountability Partners (Chapters 6-10): Left blank in the table. A Wild Card in this discussion.

A non-trivial percentage of men in the Church will now likely not need the aid of an accountability partner/group once they learn how to step up the degree to which they walk in the Spirit (Galatians 5:16). These individuals will check (√) the third box, "No Accountability Partner/Group."

Some may wish to experience the benefits of the *Way of Escape* Battle Plan while also still receiving the support and camaraderie of a partner/group. This is easily accomplished, as the Spirit-anointed apps can be seamlessly incorporated into any accountability-based purity program. These individuals will check (√) one of the first two boxes under Accountability Partners.

Others, having had their minds renewed, may still wish to be held accountable for the extra layer of protection it provides. These will also check (√) one of the first two boxes under Accountability Partners.

Family Structure #3: Blank (to be filled in by the interested reader for his unique situation).

PRAYING THE PROMISES OF GOD

Let us hold fast the confession of our hope without wavering, for He who promised is faithful (Hebrews 10:23).

Sometimes we have not, simply because we ask not (James 4:2). At other times, prayers can go unanswered because we ask amiss, with improper motives (James 4:3). Hear what noted preacher and Bible Commentator, Matthew Henry, has to say concerning rightly offered prayers:

> The best we can say to God in prayer is what He has said to us. God's promises... furnish us with the best petitions, so they are the firmest ground of our hopes, and furnish us with the best pleas.[1]

God is faithful to keep His promises (Hebrews 10:23). Praying the promises of God therefore affords us the best opportunity of having our prayers heard/answered in heaven. All fleshly desires and motives are stripped away. God's promises tell us both what to ask for and how to ask aright.

This chapter gathers together key Scripture passages that deal with avoiding/escaping sin and temptation. Passages describing the Holy Spirit's role in engineering the escape are also included. The embedded promises are extracted and tailored specifically to sexual sins and temptations. These promises are then woven together into a suggested prayer—*A Prayer for Sexual Purity.*

Six (6) key Scripture passages promising temptation avoidance or escape are gathered and then listed in the order in which they appear in the prayer that closes this chapter:

1) Promised Way of Escape from Temptation

No temptation has overtaken you except such as is common to man; but God is faithful, who will not allow you to be tempted beyond what you are able, but with the temptation will also make the way of escape, that you may be able to bear it (I Corinthians 10:13).

2) Promised Spirit-Deliverance from the Flesh

I say then: Walk in the Spirit, and you shall not fulfill the lust of the flesh (Galatians 5:16).

3) Promised Drop in Enemy "Incomings"

Therefore submit to God. Resist the devil and he will flee from you. Draw near to God and He will draw near to you ... (James 4:7-8a)

4) Promised Better Outcome if "Temptation Avoidance" Practiced

"Watch and pray, lest you enter into temptation. The spirit indeed is willing, but the flesh is weak (Matthew 26:41)."

5) Promised Mighty Weapons for Pulling Down Strongholds

For though we walk in the flesh, we do not war according to the flesh. For the weapons of our warfare are not carnal but mighty in God for pulling down strongholds (II Corinthians 10:3-4)

6) Promised Crown for Those That Endure Temptation

My brethren, count it all joy when you fall into various trials, Knowing that the testing of your faith produces patience. But let

patience have its perfect work, that you may be perfect and complete, lacking nothing ...Blessed is the man who endures temptation; for when he has been approved, he will receive the crown of life which the Lord has promised to those who love Him (James 1:2-4, 12).

Combining the preceding six (6) passages of Scripture, and claiming their embedded promises, *A Prayer for Sexual Purity* might read something like the following. Note the lengths taken to praise the oft-neglected, oft-misunderstood Third Person in the Trinity, the Holy Spirit, for His central role in engineering the escape.

A Prayer for Sexual Purity

Thanks, Praise, Confession, and Petition: I thank and praise you, gracious and loving Heavenly Father, for the many precious promises contained in your Word. I confess to having gotten careless in my walk; to having failed to remove all things in my life that have even a hint of the flesh.[2] I stopped short of Your Standards, particularly in the areas of _____, _____, and _____. To my horror, I have discovered that I cannot now break free from these sexual sins, no matter how hard I try. Deliver me from this prison of my own making. I cannot do this on my own. I have tried and failed too many times to count. My deliverance must come from you, Almighty God.

1) There is a Way of Escape: You have promised that there is a way of escape from every temptation (**I Corinthians 10:13**). I lay claim to your promise of escape, specifically from the sexual sins of _____, _____, and _____ that have so often overtaken me. Show me that promised way of escape, crafted and uniquely fitted to me and my addictions, that I might once again walk in the light, and reclaim my role as a leader, both in my home, and in the Church.

2) The Holy Spirit Leads the Escape: You have also promised that, so long as I am "walking in the Spirit," I will not fulfill the lust of the flesh (**Galatians 5:16**). I have read this verse dozens of times, but have never understood its full implications until now. Only now am I understanding that You have charged the Holy Spirit with leading the escape promised in I Corinthians 10:13. I claim the promise of Galatians 5:16, and ask that You would show me, in clear and specific detail, how to rightly "walk in the Spirit," that I might be able to consistently turn back attacks of the flesh, and make good my escape.

3) Feed the Spirit, and the Flesh Must Flee: O, the great and wonderful promises contained in your Word! You have further promised that, if I will resist the devil, and draw nigh unto You, the devil *must* flee (**James 4:7-8a**). Each time that I choose to "walk in the Spirit," I am creating healthier neural pathways that will, in time, eventually free me from even the most deeply rooted of my sexual sins. Heavenly Father, You are worthy of my unending praise. Two thousand years before the emergence of neuroscience, Your Word had already drawn up the plans for my escape. My faith in an escape is growing. I now confidently claim the promise of James 4:7-8a, believing that, by stepping up the degree to which I am walking in the Spirit, I am about to experience a dramatic drop in the number of enemy "incomings."

4) Temptation Avoidance is Key: Your Word carries an implied promise of even more dramatic drops in enemy "incomings" for those who commit to watch and pray. Jesus did not say "watch and pray to *defeat* temptation," but rather, "watch and pray to *avoid* temptation (**Matthew 26:41a**)" I claim the implied promise of reduced "incomings," given to those that practice "temptation avoidance." And I will do my part, by being careful to steer clear of those situations and places that have caused me to stumble in the past.

5) Spiritual Weaponry is Key: I thank you all-wise Heavenly Father, for, knowing the battle that I would face, You have even provided me with all the mighty weapons of spiritual warfare needed to accomplish my escape (**II Corinthians 10:3-4**). Past attempts to break free from my sexual sins have failed because they had traces of carnality, relying too much upon me, and my fleshly strength. Now relying solely on the Holy Spirit and His mighty weaponry to accomplish my escape, I lay claim to Your promise that enemy strongholds are about to come down. And in much less time than it took me to erect them. I praise and thank you Heavenly Father for Your tender mercies. Surely they are, as promised, new every morning (Lamentations 3:22-23).

6) A Crown Awaits (James 1:2-4, 12): Until now, the present trial has produced mostly shame and sadness, and very little joy. But because my brain remains plastic until death, I believe that that is about to change. Instead of Internet porn and the junk of cable TV, I am going to begin feeding my brain a steady diet of Spirit-anointed apps throughout the day as my schedule permits. And for at least 30 minutes each evening before retiring. Once again claiming the promises of Scripture (e.g., James 4:7-8a, Matthew 26:41a, and II Corinthians 10:3-4), I am trusting that, within only weeks/months, I will begin to see a significant decline in the number of attacks of the flesh. Understanding that my plastic brain is constantly undergoing neurological change, and further encouraged by knowing that others have traveled down this same road to freedom, for the first time in years/decades I am daring to believe that I am about to experience the beginnings of this same freedom. Unthinkable just weeks/months ago, I am now daring to count it all joy in the present trial (v. 2), daring to believe that, if I do allow this trial to produce patience (v. 3), and do let patience run its full course, that, just as You have promised, I too may be perfect and complete, lacking nothing (v. 4) in my battle with the flesh. Unthinkable just weeks/months ago, I believe that the promised crown of life, given to all who, out of a sincere love for Christ, patiently endure temptation, is within my grasp (v. 12). Thank you, Heavenly Father for your longsuffering patience with me. Surely You are worthy of my unending praise.

In the strong, and incomparable, and lovely name of Jesus. Amen.

FOR THE 83 PERCENT

**You are my hiding place; You shall preserve me from trouble;
You shall surround me with songs of deliverance.
(Psalm 32:7)**

In the Author Foreword, and again in Chapter 6, I claim that most Christian men will opt out of an accountability-based purity program once made aware that they must spill their sexual sins in a group setting. This seems rather obvious. It hardly seems necessary that a survey question be asked to support this claim. But such a survey question has been asked. More than simply stating the obvious, such a claim can be verified—and even quantified.

In a survey of persons wanting to quit porn, participants were asked whether they had anyone in their life helping them to quit. 83% of respondents confessed to having no one.[1] For all the success that accountability-based purity programs are reporting—and no one is disputing these reports—the simple truth is that a whopping 83% of persons wanting to quit porn are not enlisting the aid of an accountability partner/group to help them quit. It is for the 83% that *A Way of Escape* was written.

Percentage-wise, 83% of persons (5-of-6) wanting to quit porn are not seeking the help of an accountability partner/group to help them quit. But what are we talking about in terms of sheer numbers of persons? A few thousand? Maybe even a few tens of thousands?

Let's do some quick math. One organization alone reports that over 2 million men have gone through their accountability-based purity program.[2] But only one of every six persons (1-of-6) wanting help are seeking the help of an accountability partner or group. There thus remains an estimated *minimum* of 10 million (= 5 x 2 million) persons still longing for a way of escape that does not require enlisting the aid of an accountability partner or group. There thus remains an estimated *minimum* of 10 million persons still longing to be surrounded with songs of deliverance (Psalm 32:7).

> *There remains an estimated* minimum *of 10 million persons still longing for a way of escape that does not require enlisting the aid of an accountability partner or group.*

Why a *minimum* of 10 million persons? The organization cited above, while certainly boasting the largest number of followers, is not the only entity offering accountability-based help. Additionally, while the majority of sufferers are male, this is not an issue affecting only men. The 2 million men number cited above is therefore only a *lower* bound on the total number of persons that have sought accountability-based help. The estimated 10 million persons still longing for a way of escape that does not require enlisting the aid of an accountability partner/group is therefore also only a *lower* bound.

WHY AREN'T OTHERS TEACHING SPIRIT-LED ESCAPE FROM THOSE HARD-TO-ERADICATE LINGERING SINS?

I say then: Walk in the Spirit, and you shall not fulfill the lust of the flesh (Galatians 5:16).

Others *are* teaching Spirit-led escape from those hard-to-eradicate lingering sins. Some very prominent others. And they have been teaching it for a number of years. Hear what three of America's most beloved pastors have to say on this matter of lingering sins and God's provision for eradicating them.

In a 2015 sermon entitled "Walking in the Holy Spirit," Charles Stanley had this to say with regard to the Holy Spirit's power to deliver believers from lusts of the flesh (Galatians 5:16):

> *He came to do in us, and through us, and for us, what you and I could never do ourselves.*[1]

In his 2009 New York Times best-seller, *Forgotten God*, Francis Chan lists a number of things that should be a part of the believer's life if the Spirit dwells within. Pertinent to the present discussion, he had this to say with regard to the power of the Spirit to put to death the misdeeds of the body (Romans 8:2-4, 12-13):

> **The Spirit sets us free from the sins we cannot get rid of on our own.**[2]

In his 1991 New Testament Commentary on believers fulfilling the righteous requirements of the law (Romans 8:1-4), John MacArthur likens God's saving of a sinner to a courtroom transaction. As the saved sinner exits the courtroom, God hands him the code of life, and says:

> **"Now you have in you My Spirit, whose power will enable you to fulfill My law's otherwise impossible demands."** [3]

In his 1987 commentary on Galatians 5:16, MacArthur even goes so far as to say that, "All a believer ... needs to live a holy life ... is the Holy Spirit."[4]

Three of America's most beloved pastors are teaching their flocks that it is not so out of the ordinary to have a lingering sin or two that requires the *help* of the Holy Spirit *Helper* (John 16:7) to eradicate. Game-changing theology for the genuinely born-again believer still struggling to fully overcome an addiction. Game-changing theology—with the promise of a life-changing walk—if followed through to its logical "Galatians 5:16 conclusion."

> **I say then: Walk in the Spirit, and you shall not fulfill the lust of the flesh (Galatians 5:16).**

MY LIBRARY OF
GAITHER HOMECOMING
CONCERT DVDS

... be filled with the Spirit, Speaking to one another in psalms and hymns and spiritual songs, singing and making melody in your heart to the Lord (Ephesians 5:18b-19).

I was saved in 1989. I had certainly heard of the Gaithers. I was singing some of their songs during worship services in the 1990s. But until I began researching Spirit-anointed apps for this work (over the 2017 July Fourth Weekend), I was unaware of the vast treasure trove of spiritual resources that they had produced to aid believers (*all* believers, not just the senior crowd) in their walk. To my great loss, had I not written this book, I may have remained forever unaware. How many other brothers-in-arms are similarly unaware? It is my hope and prayer, therefore, that this book will help to introduce a whole new group of believers to a marvelous resource—the Gaither Homecoming concert series—for aiding and encouraging believers *of all ages* in their walk. What a high honor and privilege for me to offer such a wonderful resource to my readers.

This chapter lists entries in my library of Spirit-anointed apps taken from the Gaither Homecoming concert series (table below). All told, including compilation videos and assorted specials, the Gaithers produced over 100 of these Homecoming DVDs (*). I do not pretend to have uncovered all the flesh-obliterating gems, or even the 16 best, for I screened only 53 Homecoming concert DVDs for this work. More gems lie buried, waiting to be discovered. It is hoped, however, that the table to follow will at least provide each reader with a good starting point for their own research.

(*) A tip of the hat to Mr. Wayne Miller. Oftentimes, the first step in my search for that next addition to my library of Spirit-anointed apps was to consult his chronological track-by-track listing of Gaither Homecoming concert DVDs. A listing that could also be searched by artist, or song title.[1]

TRACKS	HOMECOMING CONCERT DVD TITLE	FAVORITE SPIRIT-ANOINTED APPS
30	Homecoming (1991)	
38	Landmark (1994)	
26	All Day Singin' and Dinner on the Ground (1995)	I Am Not Ashamed
31	Revival (1995)	
30	Holy Ground Moments of Worship and Praise (1995)	
28	Something Beautiful (1996)	
26	Sing Your Blues Away (1996)	
36	Homecoming Texas Style (1996)	
26	Joy in the Camp (1997)	Master of the Wind
		The Night Before Easter
26	Feelin' at Home (1997)	Yes, I Know
24	This is My Story (1997)	
31	Down by the Tabernacle (1998)	
21	Singin' with the Saints (1998)	
22	Rivers of Joy (1998)	He Saw Me
24	Marching to Zion (1998)	Another Soldier's Coming Home
30	All Day Singin' at the Dome (1998)	
35	Atlanta (1998)	
29	Singin' in My Soul (1999)	
24	So Glad! (1999)	
25	Sweet, Sweet Spirit (1999)	
42	Kennedy Center (1999)	I've Just Seen Jesus
26	Good News (2000)	Except for Grace
28	Harmony in the Heartland (2000)	
24	What a Time! (2000)	
33	Memphis (2000)	
35	Oh, My, Glory! (2000)	
34	Irish (2000)	
36	Whispering Hope (2000)	Then Came the Morning
27	Christmas: A Time for Joy (2001)	
22	London (2001)	The Old Rugged Cross Made the Difference

24	Journey to the Sky (2001)	
24	Passin' the Faith Along (2001)	
23	Freedom Band (2001)	
29	I'll Fly Away (2002)	Four Days Late
29	New Orleans (2002)	Through the Fire
28	God Bless America (2002)	
29	Let Freedom Ring (2002)	A Few Good Men
		Let Freedom Ring
26	Australian (2003)	
25	Red Rocks (2003)	
27	Rocky Mountain (2003)	
27	Israel (2005)	
22	Jerusalem (2005)	
24	South African (2007)	Worthy the Lamb
26	Love Can Turn the World (2007)	
18	Amazing Grace (2007)	
18	How Great Thou Art (2007)	
27	Nashville (2009)	
24	Joy in My Heart (2009)	
24	Count Your Blessings (2010)	
20	Giving Thanks (2010)	
27	The Old Rugged Cross (2011)	
25	Tent Revival (2011)	He's Alive
26	Give the World a Smile (2017)	
1441 TRACKS	**53 HOMECOMING CONCERT DVDS**	**16 FAVORITE SPIRIT-ANOINTED APPS**

NOTE: Most all Homecoming concert DVDs listed above are still available for purchase on *Amazon*, or at www.gaither.com.

Track Count: Personal testimonies are extremely powerful and are often used by the Holy Spirit to draw the hearer/viewer into His presence. Comedy/laughter may aid others in short-circuiting the flesh. At times, the visuals accompanying the Closing Credits may even help to recall a particularly touching moment from earlier tracks. My "Tracks" count (see preceding table) therefore includes all tracks listed in the DVD Menu, from Program Openings to Closing Credits, and all the testimonies, tributes, comedy sketches, narratives, conversations, readings, and instrumentals in between.

Starter Library: Some readers may be thinking, "I would like to have some level of confidence that this is going to work for me before I start shelling out the big bucks to build a 53-DVD library." Good news for the financially prudent. The following "Starter Library" of three Homecoming concert DVDs includes six of my Top 16 Spirit-anointed apps (#1, #9, #10, #11, #12, and #15):

- *Let Freedom Ring* (#1, #15)
- *The Best of Janet Paschal from the Homecoming Series* (#11, #12)
- *Joy in the Camp* (#9, #10)

Alternatively, financially prudent readers can also take a *free* "test drive" by simply going to the *YouTube* website and previewing the playlists for the Homecoming concert DVDs listed above.

Nightly Mind Renewal: I keep my mind renewed by regularly viewing Spirit-anointed, flesh-diffusing apps for 30-60 minutes most evenings. A favorite playlist follows. All entries are from the *Tent Revival* Homecoming Concert DVD[2], which makes for easy, uninterrupted viewing. A tribute to the Billy Graham crusades dating to the 1950s, some of the artists even dressed in period clothing. The clothes might have changed, but the Spirit's anointing is the same. Sit back, and bask in His presence.

Close Encounters of the Son and Spirit Kind
from the *Tent Revival* Homecoming Concert
(approximately 28 minutes)

Yes, I Know	Honoring the Son
I Stand Amazed	Marvelous the Savior's Love
Down to the River to Pray	Jesus: The Way to a Crown
The Ninety and Nine	Tender Shepherd Tribute
More Than Ever	The Cross: For You and Me!
Lord, I'm Coming Home	The Spirit Gently Woos
He's Alive	The Spirit Unleashed. Wow!

All entries in this second playlist are from *The Best of Janet Paschal from the Homecoming Series*.[3] In his introductory remarks, Mr. Gaither describes how Ms. Paschal can "disarm the roughest and toughest members of an audience." Another has said, "she could sing the phone book and I'd be blessed." Not many better ways to calm one's mind from the events of the day. Dear reader, watch and be blessed by the Spirit.

Calming, Spirit-Anointed Songs to Inspire and Bless
from *The Best of Janet Paschal from the Homecoming Series*
(approximately 33 minutes)

I Am Not Ashamed ....Arresting. Inspiring. Wow!
God Will Make a Way ....If This Book Was a Song
Another Soldier's Coming Home .. Heart-Tugs Abound
Written in Red ....Calming. Beautiful.
The Body and the Blood ....Comfort for the Broken
How are Things at Home? ....Grief-Relieving App
You're Still Lord ....Love Song to the Lord

A third playlist follows. All entries are from the *Let Freedom Ring* Homecoming Concert DVD.[4] A good mix of patriotism and a spiritual call to arms. This playlist occupies a special place in my heart, for it was a Spirit-filling experienced while watching *A Few Good Men* over the 2017 July Fourth Weekend that inspired the writing of this book.

A Good Mix of Patriotism and a Spiritual Call to Arms
from the *Let Freedom Ring* Homecoming Concert
(approximately 23 minutes)

God Bless the USA ....Patriotic Classic
When He Calls I'll Fly Away ....Southern Gospel Classic
More Than Wonderful ....Love This Classic Duo
A Few Good Men ....My #1 Spirit-Anointed App
Let Freedom Ring ....Power Anthem. Wow!

A fourth and final playlist follows. All entries are from the *Good News* Homecoming Concert DVD[5] which, once more, makes for easy, uninterrupted viewing.

Good Fun, Good Theology, and Good Music
from the *Good News* Homecoming Concert
(approximately 31 minutes)

Trying to Get a Glimpse ....Christians Having Fun!
The Ninety and Nine ....Tender Shepherd Tribute
Narrative ....The Good News
I'm Free .... Celebratory Reflection
When He Set Me Free ....More Christian Fun!
Lord, Feed Your Children ....Heart-Tugs
Narrative ....What the Church Should Be
Except for Grace ....More Heart-Tugs

As often as I have viewed these playlists, they never get old and never lose their anointing. Apps with infinite shelf life that may be accessed, and immersed in, at any time I desire to experience the intimate, sheltering presence of the Spirit. The promises of God are true, and never fail. As promised, so long as I continue to draw from His bottomless well, I need never again be spiritually thirsty (John 4:13-14). Thank you, Holy Spirit!

Babies and Bath Water: No one captures movings of the Spirit on camera better than the Gaither Music Group. No one (see *The "John 3:8ers,"* Chapter 7). Watch that you do not throw the babies out with the bath water. Watch that you do not throw the earlier Gaither Homecoming apps (my apps 7-12) out with the 1990s leisure suits and hairstyles. A Good Reminder: It's not about the hair and suits. It's all about the Holy Spirit!

It's not about the hair and suits.
It's all about the Holy Spirit!

ESCAPE IN FIVE EASY STEPS

No temptation has overtaken you except such as is common to man; but God is faithful, who will not allow you to be tempted beyond what you are able, but with the temptation will also make the way of escape, that you may be able to bear it.
(I Corinthians 10:13)

I, _____, am currently experiencing approximately ____ attacks of the flesh per month, followed by approximately ____ episodes of "acting out" per month. Enough! Dropping the passivity, I am ready to claim the way of escape promised in I Corinthians 10:13. I am ready to try the *Way of Escape* Battle Plan.

Signature: _____   Date: _____

Step 1. Identify and Exercise Spiritual Gifts (Chapter 3)
Step 2. Remove the Offending Eye (Chapter 4)
Step 3. Watch and Pray (Chapter 5)
Step 4. Build Library of Spirit-Anointed Apps (Chapters 6-7)

Readers already practicing the spiritual disciplines described in Steps 1-3 may begin at Step 4. (But only if you have been diligent in practicing Steps 1-3. Do not skip steps. Do not complete steps 1-3 half-heartedly). Other readers may require several months simply to complete Step 1. Timelines will be a function of each reader's unique history and circumstances.

Before I began to collect data, I spent 5-1/2 months screening candidates for inclusion in my library of Spirit-anointed, flesh-diffusing apps (Step 4). On my Kickoff Date for the start of data collection (December 15, 2017), I had added 12 of the 23 apps that would eventually comprise my finished library. But I started from scratch. Readers gain the benefit of my experience. They will have access to my finished library. Most readers should therefore be able to construct a library of 10 or so apps in a time period significantly shorter than my 5-1/2 months.

Kickoff Date for Start of Data Collection: _____

What to include in the notes following the table (page opposite)? That will be a function of each individual's unique experience. But at a minimum, readers might want to document:

- Initial AF/month and AO/month rates prior to starting on the *Way of Escape* Battle Plan
- When enemy "incomings" began to reduce in number
- When enemy "incomings" began to reduce in strength
- Date of the final episode of "acting out"
- When complete mind renewal was achieved (*not* the same date as the final episode of "acting out;" there is typically a time lag between this final episode and achieving complete mind renewal)
- Final AF/month and AO/month rates

STEP 5
Attacks of the Flesh (AF)
and Episodes of Acting Out (AO)
Over the Last ___ Months

Year	Month	Days	AF	AO		Year	Month	Days	AF	AO
202_	January					202_	January			
	February						February			
	March						March			
	April						April			
Attacks	May					Attacks	May			
___	June					___	June			
	July						July			
	August						August			
Acted	September					Acted	September			
Out	October					Out	October			
___	November					___	November			
	December						December			
202_	January					202_	January			
	February						February			
	March						March			
	April						April			
Attacks	May					Attacks	May			
___	June					___	June			
	July						July			
	August						August			
Acted	September					Acted	September			
Out	October					Out	October			
___	November					___	November			
	December						December			
							TOTALS			

Table Highlights and Notes:

161

WHY "WALKING IN THE SPIRIT" WORKS

I say then: Walk in the Spirit, and you shall not fulfill the lust of the flesh (Galatians 5:16).

Biblical Explanation: Why does "walking in the Spirit" work? The best and shortest answer? Because it is instruction coming directly from the Word of God (Galatians 5:16).

Of course, "because the Bible says so" is the best answer. But for the benefit of those (author included) that receive a faith boost each time Scripture anticipates a scientific discovery, the question is rephrased.

Neurological Explanation: From a neurological perspective, why does "walking in the Spirit" work? Let's first hear noted psychiatrist and "neuroplastician" Dr. Norman Doidge's take on mind renewal in the related case of persons with obsessive-compulsive brain disorders:

> *With this treatment we don't so much "break" bad habits as replace bad behaviors with better ones.*[1]

Doidge's take on mind renewal makes perfect brain-plasticity sense. The replacement behavior creates a new (better) brain circuit. In dopamine-related neuroscience discussions, "better" is equivalent to "more pleasurable." That being said, if the brain's owner does indeed find the replacement behavior to be more pleasurable, it will be repeated often. And each time it is repeated, the new (better) brain circuit strengthens. This new (better) circuit can now compete with the older (bad) one and eventually replace it.

Neurologically speaking, "walking in the Spirit" works according to these same principles. "Walking in the Spirit" works by replacing bad behaviors with better and more pleasurable ones. The bad experience of viewing porn is replaced with the better and more pleasurable experience of immersing oneself in the Spirit-anointed, flesh-diffusing apps. For the genuinely born-again believer, having the Spirit well up within while viewing a rousing rendition of *Where No One Stands Alone*,[2] is a better and more pleasurable experience than viewing a pornographic video.

> **For the genuinely born-again believer, having the Spirit well up within while viewing a rousing rendition of Where No One Stands Alone,[2] is a better and more pleasurable experience than viewing a pornographic video.**

Hear next what the writer of *Where No One Stands Alone* had to say to The Homecoming Friends upon hearing/experiencing their rousing rendition of his song:

> *... to hear it sung by a roomful of friends, and sung like that, is an unbelievable experience ... It just about sends me straight to heaven!*[3]

A welling up of the Spirit. An unbelievably pleasurable experience. All packed into a 3-1/2-minute music video. That, dear reader, is *both* the biblical *and* neurological explanation for why "walking in the Spirit" works.

Not surprisingly, nearly 2000 years ago, Jesus was already teaching on the need for replacement behaviors. His parable on the need to fill voids left by the departure of unclean spirits still rings true today. The house swept clean, and put in order. But if left empty, the voids will eventually be filled by spirits even more wicked than the first (Matthew 12:43-45). An eerily similar description of the porn addict trying to quit his habit cold turkey. Only to find himself caught up in a seemingly endless series of escalating binge-and-purge cycles (see *Novelty, Tolerance, and Escalation*, Chapter 2).

Non-Technical Explanation: Neuroplasticity, dopamine, and Spirit-anointed apps. Heady stuff indeed. Might there be a simpler, non-technical explanation for why "walking in the Spirit" works?

> **KEY SIMPLIFICATION**: *I become addicted to porn by repeatedly immersing myself in porn. I become addicted to the Spirit by repeatedly immersing myself in the Spirit (Galatians 5:16).*

Dear reader, you can do this. First clean house according to the guidelines provided in Chapters 3-5 (and Matthew 12:43-44). Then begin to build a library of Spirit-anointed, flesh-diffusing apps. Apps that are uniquely fitted to you, and your unique Spirit-filling triggers. Finally—and this is the really *fun* and *easy* part—simply start daily walking in your Spirit-anointed apps (Galatians 5:16).

> *I say then: Walk in the Spirit, and you shall not fulfill the lust of the flesh (Galatians 5:16).*

This new (better) circuit that you are creating now competes with the older (bad) one. In time, it will eventually replace it. For me, it really was that simple. Perhaps for you too, dear reader?

WHAT MUST I DO TO BE SAVED?

The Holy Spirit can deliver only those in whom He dwells (John 14:17). I cannot overcome the flesh by walking in the Spirit (Galatians 5:16) if I have never been born of the Spirit (John 3:3-8). At a first and most fundamental level, I must therefore examine myself, to determine whether I am truly in the faith (II Corinthians 13:5).

Scripture teaches that many will perish, and that only a relative few will inherit eternal life (Matthew 7:13-14). Accordingly, this final chapter follows two individuals named MANY and FEW (and a third named SOME, a subset of the MANY) on their journey of spiritual discovery.

The theology is first examined, followed by the "how-to" of experiencing God's Salvation. Failing to remove all things that have even a hint of the flesh may result in even those that have been genuinely born-again falling back into sexual sin.[1] To guard against this happening, special emphasis is placed on repentance in the conversion process. A common misconception held by the MANY is then addressed using five examples of salvation recorded in the Book of Acts. Finally, emphasis is placed on the work of the Holy Spirit in the conversion process. Praise God, we are not in this battle alone.

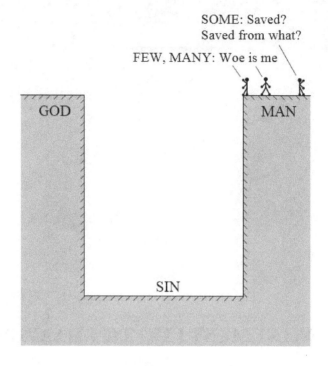

ALL ARE SINNERS

The Bible teaches that none are righteous, that all are sinners, and that our sins separate us from God:

- As it is written: "There is none righteous, no, not one (Romans 3:10)."
- For all have sinned and fall short of the glory of God (Romans 3:23).
- But your iniquities have separated you from your God; and your sins have hidden His face from you, so that He will not hear (Isaiah 59:2).

Most (the FEW and the MANY in the figure) eventually do acknowledge their sinful condition and seek to be reconciled with God. But only a relative FEW will follow biblically-correct paths and ultimately be saved, i.e., make it to heaven.

"Enter by the narrow gate; for wide is the gate and broad is the way that leads to destruction, and there are *many* who go in by it. Because narrow is the gate and difficult is the way which leads to life, and there are *few* who find it (Matthew 7:13-14)."

MANY, though indeed zealous for God, will elect to follow man-made, non-biblical paths and—tragedy-of-tragedies—miss heaven altogether. Mankind does not change. Modern man will make the same mistakes as the children of Israel. What Paul wrote to his first century countrymen, he wrote to all men of all ages:

Brethren, my heart's desire and prayer to God for Israel is that they may be saved. For I bear them witness that they have a zeal for God, but not according to knowledge. For they being ignorant of God's righteousness, and seeking to establish their own righteousness, have not submitted to the righteousness of God. For Christ is the end of the law for righteousness to everyone who believes (Romans 10:1-4).

SOME will live lives of open rebellion, never seeking to be reconciled with the God of the Bible.

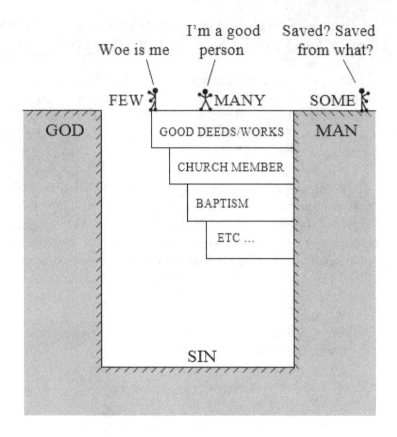

GOOD WORKS ARE INSUFFICIENT

Most (the FEW and the MANY) eventually do acknowledge their sinful condition and seek to be reconciled unto God, usually through some combination of good deeds, joining a church, and baptism. But if it were possible to be reconciled to God in this manner, then Jesus' death on the cross was all for naught. MANY even "believe" in Christ, but, if completely honest, would confess that He is filed away somewhere in the "ETC" category of their life (see figure above); thought of, and spoken of, far less than their good deeds, church affiliation, and baptism. Continuing this latter thought:

Dear reader, if you were to die today, and, standing before God, He was to ask you: "Why should I allow you into My Heaven?" what would you say? Write down your answer, and then count the mentions of good deeds, church affiliation,

170

baptism, and Jesus. In all likelihood, the item with the most mentions is what you are trusting in for your salvation. Is it Jesus? Is it—as it must be—Jesus *alone*?

Only a relative FEW realize, as the Bible teaches, that all of their good deeds are still sin-stained. These FEW understand that the "good works" and the "Jesus plus good works" approaches to God will therefore always fall short:

- But we are all like an unclean thing, and all our righteousnesses are like filthy rags ... (Isaiah 64:6)
- For by grace you have been saved through faith, and that not of yourselves; it is the gift of God, Not of works, lest anyone should boast (Ephesians 2:8-9).
- Not by works of righteousness which we have done, but according to His mercy He saved us... (Titus 3:5)

MANY, not schooled in the Bible, are deceived into believing that a loving and merciful God will accept their man-made religion of good works. Satisfied with their own self-righteousness, they no longer seek to be reconciled to God through Christ alone.

SOME remain openly rebellious, never seeking to be reconciled with the God of the Bible.

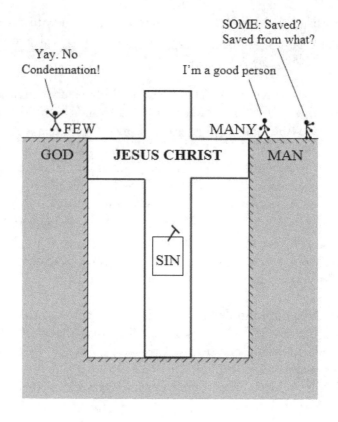

JESUS IS THE ONLY WAY

All of our good deeds are still sin-stained. The "good person" approach to God will, therefore, always fall short. But the loving and merciful God of the Bible made a Way. Because Christ lived a sinless life, when He shed His blood and died on the cross, He satisfied God's requirement for a perfect, sinless sacrifice for sin.

When a sinner trusts in Christ's shed blood alone for the forgiveness of sins, God nails their sins to the cross, i.e., He transfers their sin debt to Christ's account. At the cross, the born-again believer's sin debt is "Paid in Full." These FEW that trust in Christ alone for the forgiveness of their sin are now no longer under the condemnation of hell:

- For the wages of sin is death, but the gift of God is eternal life in Christ Jesus our Lord (Romans 6:23).
- Jesus said to him, "I am the way, the truth, and the life. No one comes to the Father except through Me (John

14:6)."

- There is therefore now no condemnation to those who are in Christ Jesus, who do not walk according to the flesh, but according to the Spirit (Romans 8:1).

All praise to the loving and merciful God of the Bible. Deserving death, instead He grants eternal life (Romans 6:23)! Deserving judgment, instead He pardons! Indeed, God is love (I John 4:8).

Tragically, MANY will reject Christ's righteousness, choosing instead to erect and trust in their own standard of righteousness. Listen again to the apostle Paul's impassioned plea to the MANY zealously religious—but unsaved—of Israel:

Brethren, my heart's desire and prayer to God for Israel is that they may be saved. For I bear them witness that they have a zeal for God, but not according to knowledge. For they being ignorant of God's righteousness, and seeking to establish their own righteousness, have not submitted to the righteousness of God. For Christ is the end of the law for righteousness to everyone who believes (Romans 10:1-4).

Mankind does not change. Modern man will make the same mistakes as the children of Israel. What Paul wrote to his first century countrymen, he wrote to all men of all ages. These MANY—both in Paul's day and today—having spent a lifetime rejecting God's loving call from the cross, condemn themselves to hell.

SOME will continue to live lives of open rebellion, never seeking to be reconciled with the God of the Bible. Tragically, these also condemn themselves to hell.

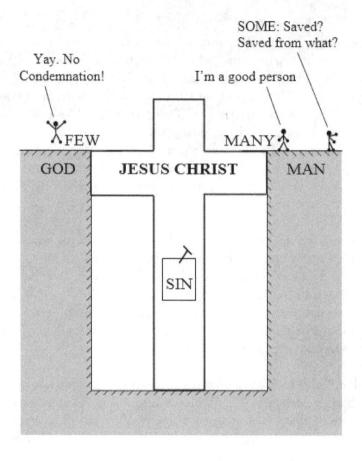

WHAT MUST I DO TO BE SAVED?

The theology thoroughly covered, just what is it that a person must actually *do* to be saved?

- **CONFESS** that I am a sinner, in need of a Savior. For all have sinned and fall short of the glory of God (Romans 3:23).
- **BELIEVE** that Jesus Christ is the *only* Savior of my soul. Jesus said to him, "I am the way, the truth, and the life. No one comes to the Father except through Me (John 14:6)."
- **REPENT**, i.e., have a change of heart and mind about sin, with a resulting change in actions. For godly sorrow produces repentance leading to salvation... (II

174

Corinthians 7:10)

- **RECEIVE** Christ as Savior and Lord. But as many as received Him, to them He gave the right to become children of God ... (John 1:12)

What does it mean to receive Christ? Is believing that Jesus is the Son of God the same as receiving Him?

Suppose that I have an incurable disease. A doctor has discovered a cure and is offering it to all, free-of-charge. I've read about the cure. I've spoken with persons who have been cured. I *believe* that it will work for me too. But unless I actually *receive* the doctor's cure, I will still die.

Similarly, it is not enough for me to read about Christ. It is not enough to hear about the good He has done for others. It is not even enough to believe that He is the Son of God, for even the demons believe (Matthew 8:29 and James 2:19). I must, in a willful act, receive Christ into my heart and life for my belief to have any saving effect.

Dear reader, ditch the man-made, works-based religions which lead only to death. Pray to receive Christ today. God knows your heart. He is not as concerned with your words, or the length of your prayer, as He is with the attitude of your heart. Pray to receive Christ into your heart and life now—before it is forever too late!

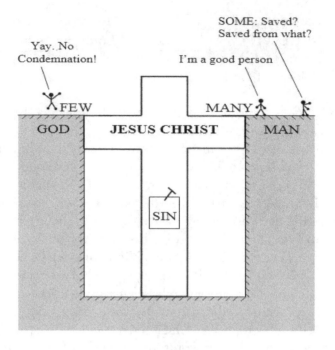

YES, IT IS THAT EASY

"No, it can't be that easy," MANY will say. "What you've described couldn't take more than an hour. There are things that I must first clean up, wrongs that I must make right, and classes that I must attend. Maybe in a month or two, or maybe next year God will accept me. It simply can't be as easy as you've described."

Oh, but it is that easy. If the Good News of Jesus Christ is explained by one skilled in the Word of God, and if received by one *already under conviction and ready to repent of their sins*, then, yes, complete conversion can occur within the hour. That's the Gospel (e.g., the *Good News*) of Jesus Christ. Listen again to Ephesians 2:8-9:

- For by grace, i.e., God's unmerited favor
- You have been saved through faith,
- And that not of yourselves, i.e., not by cleaning yourself up
- It is the gift of God,
- Not of works, i.e., not by making wrongs right, or by taking a series of classes
- Lest anyone should boast

176

Still having trouble believing that it can be that easy? As if anticipating the difficulty that MANY might have comprehending salvation by grace through faith, God provided five examples of start-to-finish conversions in the Book of Acts to which timelines can be attached:

1. At Peter's Pentecostal Sermon, 3,000 souls went from asking "Men and brethren, what shall we do (to be saved)?" to being added to the church, all in the space of a *single day* (Acts 2:37-41)

2. The Ethiopian eunuch went from being unable to comprehend the Scriptures, to being saved, in the time (maybe *an hour?*) it took Philip to overtake his chariot, preach Jesus to him, and baptize him (Acts 8:26-39)

3. Saul went from persecuting the church, to being baptized into Christ, all in the space of *three days* (Acts 9:1-18)

4. Cornelius (and his company) went from being a Gentile still outside the church, to being baptized into Christ, all in the space of *four days* (Acts 10:30-48)

5. The Philippian jailor went from asking "Sirs, what must I do to be saved?" to being baptized (with his entire family) into Christ, all in the *same hour* of the night (Acts 16:30-34)

What shall we say then of good deeds/works, if start-to-finish biblical conversions require no more than an hour to several days? They must be a *product* of salvation, not the means of salvation (Ephesians 2:8-10).

Ye Must Be Born Again

Jesus answered and said to him, "Most assuredly, I say to you, unless one is born again, he cannot see the kingdom of God (John 3:3)."

NO, IT IS NOT *THAT* EASY

I know what some are thinking: *Eternal life within the hour. I'll have some of that. Sign me up.*

No, it is not *that* easy. In varying ways, the Scriptures make it clear that true conversion always results in a changed life:

- "But why do you call Me 'Lord, Lord,' and not do the things which I say (Luke 6:46)?"
- "I tell you, no; but unless you repent you will all likewise perish (Luke 13:3)."
- Jesus answered and said to him, "Most assuredly, I say to you, unless one is born again, he cannot see the kingdom of God (John 3:3)."
- But be doers of the word, and not hearers only, deceiving

yourselves (James 1:22).

- You believe that there is one God. You do well. Even the demons believe—and tremble! But do you ... know, O foolish man, that faith without works is dead (James 2:19-20)?

These are five different ways of communicating the same Spiritual Truth: Faith that fails to produce a changed life is not saving faith.

It is true that, because we are saved through faith, and not by works, it is much easier to be saved than MANY believe. However, it is not easy, at least not in one's own power. But all praise to God. Upon receiving Christ, the Holy Spirit provides the inner power to turn from sin (Ephesians 3:20), enabling the child of God to now walk in a manner that is pleasing to God (Romans 8:1-4).

Conclusion: We are saved by grace through faith, and not by works. But faith without works is dead. So which is it: works, or no works? Ephesians 2:10 is the key to resolving this apparent contradiction: We are saved, not by faith *plus* works, but by a faith *that* works:

For by grace you have been saved through faith, and that not of yourselves; it is the gift of God, Not of works, lest anyone should boast. For we are His workmanship, created in Christ Jesus for good works, which God prepared beforehand that we should walk in them (Ephesians 2:8-10).

INDEX

SCRIPTURE INDEX
(Through Appendix G only)

The letters f, n, or t following a page number
denote a figure, note, or table

SUBJECT INDEX
(Through Appendix G only)

The letters f, n, or t following a page number
denote a figure, note, or table

About Kharis Publishing:

Kharis Publishing, an imprint of Kharis Media LLC, is a leading Christian and inspirational book publisher based in Aurora, Chicago metropolitan area, Illinois. Kharis' dual mission is to give voice to under-represented writers (including women and first-time authors) and equip orphans in developing countries with literacy tools. That is why, for each book sold, the publisher channels some of the proceeds into providing books and computers for orphanages in developing countries, so that these kids may learn to read, dream, and grow. For a limited time, Kharis Publishing is accepting unsolicited queries for nonfiction (Christian, self-help, memoirs, business, health and wellness) from qualified leaders, professionals, pastors, and ministers. Learn more at: About Us - Kharis Publishing - Accepting Manuscript

CPSIA information can be obtained
at www.ICGtesting.com
Printed in the USA
BVHW040311010422
632940BV00006B/18